T0193602

BEFORE
THE
FLOOD

Paul J. Arnold

Cover Design by Kati Gilbert

WESTBOW
PRESS®
A DIVISION OF THOMAS NELSON
& ZONDERVAN

WestBow Press books may be ordered through booksellers or by contacting:

WestBow Press
A Division of Thomas Nelson & Zondervan
1663 Liberty Drive
Bloomington, IN 47403
www.westbowpress.com
844-714-3454

Scripture taken from the New King James Version® Copyright © 1982 by Thomas Nelson. Used by permission. All rights reserved.

ISBN: 978-1-6642-3122-1 (sc)
ISBN: 978-1-6642-3121-4 (hc)
ISBN: 978-1-6642-3123-8 (e)

Library of Congress Control Number: 2021907835

Print information available on the last page.

WestBow Press rev. date: 05/13/2021

Dedication

1. I dedicate this book to my mother, Debra, a retired French and History teacher of 30 plus years of service. Thanks for always having my back, even when I fall down. I love you!
2. This book is also dedicated to all those who have sought the truth about our past.

Contents

"'Let not your heart be troubled; you believe in God, believe also in Me. In My Father's house are many mansions; if it were not so, I would have told you. I go to prepare a place for you. And if I go and prepare a place for you, I will come again and receive you to Myself; that where I am, there you may be also. And where I go you know, and the way you know'. Thomas said to Him, 'Lord, we do not know where You are going, and how can we know the way?' Jesus said to him, **'I am the way, the truth, and the life. No one comes to the Father except through Me'**." – John 14: 1–6

Information

- All quoted Bible verses come from the New King James Version.
- To avoid any confusion, all bracketed [] Bible verses are for comparable purposes only as to what was just examined.
- You will notice that I do NOT capitalize the 's' in the adversary's name. To capitalize a noun means to give it proper attention. The devil does not deserve that kind of attention.
- All parentheses found in the source itself are of my doing, with the exception of one found in the Creation chapter. Those parentheses are from Dr. Wise himself.
- The cubit was a unit of measurement in the days of old, it is approximately 18 inches, the length of one's forearm.
- The shekel was a unit of measurement in ancient Israel and equals roughly 11 grams – so it would take roughly 2.5 shekels to equal an ounce and 38 shekels to equal one pound.

Foreword

"HiStory is a great way to know HIM." ~ Paul J. Arnold

Google the word obsession and this is what you get: *an idea or thought that continually preoccupies or intrudes on a person's mind.*

This is how it is shown used in a sentence: *"<u>he was in the grip of an obsession he was powerless to resist</u>".*

Ironic…that sentence is exactly what I would say about my friend Paul and his obsession with history, namely biblical history. If you want to see his eyes twinkle and his ears perk up, ask a question about history. There is no doubt that Paul approaches the topic with unparalleled zeal and excitement. To say he is well read is an understatement, and this book is his labor of love…a decade in the making.

2020 has been quite the year. A global pandemic, racial tension, unrest and injustice, riots, a divisive election, etc.…Sometimes as a society it seems we take 2 steps forward and 3 steps back. The more things change the more they stay the same. History repeats itself. Our time could be a chapter in the old testament. I often hear that our world is "going to hades in a handbasket". And where is our hope?

Paul has always intimated that he knows the unseen binding agent of history…ALL of history. This book bridges the history of multiple cultures by overlaying them side by side with the Bible, revealing an astounding secret, and that there is hope.

So, my advice is to not skip the preface and do not skim over the bibliography. Grab a cup of coffee and a highlighter. And get ready to see history through a new lens with a surprising twist.

Craig Thompson

November 2020

Preface

History, or at least what we think we know about ancient times, is stories passed down orally from generation to generation until someone with the ability to write it down does so. The term itself comes from the Greek word *historia*, meaning to inquire or investigate. It can also be defined as the study of written documents. As I have told the college students that I was privileged to teach for a while at my home church, "Legends come from somewhere, they were not just fabricated out of thin air", and I would also tell them, "Do your own research".

Now, before I get into the reasoning behind the sources for the purpose of this book, let us cover some definitions first. All of these definitions can be found in the Merriam-Webster dictionary on-line. They are as follows:

Canon – a regulation or dogma decreed by a church council; an authoritative list of books accepted as Holy Scripture; a sanctioned or accepted group or body of related works.

Deuterocanonical – of, relating to, or constituting the books of Scripture contained in the Septuagint but not in the Hebrew canon.

Apocrypha – writings or statements of dubious authenticity; books included in the Septuagint and Vulgate but excluded from the Jewish and Protestant canons of the Old Testament; early Christian writings not included in the New Testament.

Pseudepigrapha – any of various pseudonymous or anonymous Jewish religious writings of the period 200 BC – 200 AD; such writings not included in any canon of Biblical Scripture.

Apocrypha literally means 'hidden things' when translated from Greek and deuterocanonical literally means 'secondary canon'. These types of books form two categories; those that have been included in some canonical versions of the Bible, and those that are biblical in nature but have never been canonized for some reason or another, probably due to textual and doctrinal issues. In fact, the Roman Catholic Church installed part of the apocrypha/deuterocanonical writings (seven to be exact) to its Bible in the 1500s, and even in America, some seminary schools use this Bible.

The sources that I have chosen to use for this book are the ***Book of Jubilees***, the ***Book of Jasher***, ***The Legends of the Jews***, the ***First and Second Books of Adam and Eve***, and, of course, the ***Book of Enoch***. All of these writings fall into either the deuterocanonical or pseudepigrapha by definition and nature. However, the ***Book of Jasher*** and ***The Legends of the Jews*** are both more historical narratives than the others. We need to investigate and consider the other books not in the Bible because the writers of the Bible did so. Portions, if not all, of these books were found in the caves of Qumran in 1948 and are now part of what has come to be called the Dead Sea Scrolls. The only parts of these works in use for the purpose of this book are those that speak of what happened before the Great Flood.

Joseph B. Lumpkin tells us, "The Bible can direct us to other works in three ways. The work can be mentioned by name, as is the Book of Jasher. The work can be quoted within the Bible text, as is the case with the Book of Enoch. The existence of the work can be alluded to, as is the case of the missing letter from the apostle Paul to the Corinthians."[1] Here is a list of thirteen books listed by name in the Bible in order of appearance:

1. *The Book of the Wars of the Lord* [Numbers 21:14–15] – "Therefore it is said in the Book of the Wars of the Lord: 'Waheb in Shuphah, the brooks of the Arnon, and the slope of the brooks that reaches to the dwelling of Ar, and lies on the border of Moab'."

2. *The Book of Jasher* [Joshua 10:12–14] – "Then Joshua spoke to the Lord in the day when the Lord delivered up the Amorites before the children of Israel, and he said in the sight of Israel: 'Sun, stand still over Gibeon; and moon, in the valley of Aijalon'. So the sun stood still, and the moon stopped, till the people had revenge upon

their enemies. Is this not written in the Book of Jasher? So the sun stood still in the midst of heaven, and did not hasten to go down for about a whole day. And there has been no day like that, before it or after it, that the Lord heeded the voice of a man; for the Lord fought for Israel."

3. *Samuel's book* [1 Samuel 10:25] – "Then Samuel explained to the people the behavior of royalty, and wrote it in a book and laid it up before the Lord. And Samuel sent all the people away, every man to his house."

4. *The Acts of Solomon* [1 Kings 11:41] – "Now the rest of the acts of Solomon, all that he did, and his wisdom, are they not written in the book of the acts of Solomon?"

5. *The Chronicles of David* [1 Chronicles 27:24] – "Joab the son of Zeruiah began a census, but he did not finish, for wrath came upon Israel because of this census; nor was the number recorded in the account of the chronicles of King David."

6. *The Book of Samuel, Nathan, and Gad* [1 Chronicles 29:29–30] – "Now the acts of King David, first and last, indeed they are written in the book of Samuel the seer, in the book of Nathan the prophet, and in the book of Gad the seer, with all his reign and his might, and the events that happened to him, to Israel, and to all the kingdoms of the lands."

7. *The Book of Nathan* [2 Chronicles 9:29] – "Now the rest of the acts of Solomon, first and last, are they not written in the book of Nathan the prophet, in the prophecy of Ahijah the Shilonite, and in the visions of Iddo the seer concerning Jeroboam the son of Nebat?"

8. *The Prophecy of Ahijah the Shilonite* [2 Chronicles 9:29] – "Now the rest of the acts of Solomon, first and last, are they not written in the book of Nathan the prophet, in the prophecy of Ahijah the Shilonite, and in the visions of Iddo the seer concerning Jeroboam the son of Nebat?"

9. *The Annals of the Prophet Iddo* [2 Chronicles 13:22] – "Now the rest of the acts of Abijah, his ways, and his sayings are written in the annals of the prophet Iddo."

10. *The Book of Jehu* [2 Chronicles 20:34] – "Now the rest of the acts of Jehoshaphat, first and last, indeed they are written in the book of Jehu the son of Hanani, which is mentioned in the book of the kings of Israel."

11. *The Annals of the Book of the Kings* [2 Chronicles 24:27] – "Now concerning his sons, and the many oracles about him, and the repairing of the house of God, indeed they are written in the annals of the book of the kings. Then Amaziah his son reigned in his place."

12. *The Sayings of Hozai* [2 Chronicles 33:19] – "Also his prayer and how God received his entreaty, and all his sin and trespass, and the sites where he built high places and set up wooden images and carved images, before he was humbled, indeed they are written among the sayings of Hozai."

13. *The Book of the Records, of the Chronicles of the King* [Esther 2:23 ; 6:1] – "And when an inquiry was made into the matter, it was confirmed, and both were hanged on a gallows; and it was written in the book of the chronicles in the presence of the king." ; "That night the king could not sleep. So one was commanded to bring the book of the records of the chronicles; and they were read before the king."

The only book of these that is in existence today is the Book of Jasher. How great it would be if we had access to these books, but alas, we do not. They have been lost to history, although I am sure some have been found, but the uncertainties of their authenticity have kept them from the public eye.

The **Book of Jubilees**, or *'Little Genesis'* as it is also called, is a timeline of events from Genesis and Exodus. Ken Johnson states that it "was well known in the first century AD. It was lost to most of the Christian world for centuries, preserved only in four Ge'ez texts dating to the 15th and 16th centuries. In 1948 with the discovery of the Dead Sea Scrolls, fifteen Hebrew scroll fragments were found of the Book of Jubilees. The English text used here is from the public domain, R. H. Charles, 1917 Edition, which is based on the Ethiopic language of Ge'ez...The Book of Jubilees has some phraseology that suggests it was originally a Hebrew document translated into Greek and then into Ge'ez."[2] It falls into the pseudepigrapha category as we do not know the original author, but I do encourage those that want to read it to do so, as it has proven to be useful when studying the history of the Israelites. However, it is not as accurate as the **Book of Jasher**.

The First and Second Books of Adam and Eve, or as it is sometimes referred to, 'The Conflict of Adam and Eve with Satan', also fall into the pseudepigrapha category. These works are now considered fiction, but from the beginning of the Church they were read.

> The familiar version in Genesis is not the source of this fundamental legend, it is not a spontaneous, Heaven-born account that sprang into place in the Old Testament. It is simply a version, unexcelled perhaps, but a version of a myth or belief or account handed down by word of mouth from generation to generation of mankind – through the incoherent, unrecorded ages of man it came – like an inextinguishable ray of light that ties the time when human life began, with the time when the human mind could express itself and the human hand could write…The version which we give here is the work of unknown Egyptians (the lack of historical allusion makes it impossible to date the writing). Parts of this version are found in the Talmud, the Koran, and elsewhere, showing what a vital role it played in the original literature of human wisdom. The Egyptian author first wrote in Arabic (which may be taken as the original manuscript) and that found its way farther south and was translated into Ethiopic. For the present English translation, we are indebted to Dr. S. C. Malan, Vicar of Broadwindsor, who worked from the Ethiopic edition edited by Dr. E. Trumpp, Professor at the University of Munich. Dr. Trumpp had the advantage of the Arabic original, which makes our bridge over the gap of many centuries a direct one…One critic said of this writing: 'This is we believe, the greatest literary discovery that the world has known. Its effect upon contemporary

thought in molding the judgment of the future generations is of incalculable value. The treasures of Tut-ankh-Amen's tomb were no more precious to the Egyptologist than are these literary treasures to the world of scholarship'.[3] (Platt, *Forgotten Books*, 1–2)

The author is unknowable at this point, but I speculate that it was probably written some 300 years or so before the birth of Christ, and that is solely based upon other pseudepigraphal writings. However, today most theologians and scholars consider it to be just literature. What is known is that these books are remarkably interesting and intriguing as they are kind of like a sequel to the Adam and Eve story found in Genesis. Please do not compare the two.

The Legends of the Jews, authored by Louis Ginzberg, does not really fall into any of the categories listed above, but is a historical narrative that goes from creation to Esther. Ginzberg himself states, "In the present work, 'The Legends of the Jews', I have made the first attempt to gather from the original sources all Jewish legends, in so far as they refer to biblical personages and events, and reproduce them with the greatest attainable completeness and accuracy. I use the expression Jewish, rather than Rabbinic, because the sources which I have levied contributions are not limited to the Rabbinic literature…Jewish legends can be culled not from the writings of the Synagogue alone; they appear also in those of the Church. Certain Jewish works repudiated by the Synagogue were accepted and mothered by the Church. This is the literature usually denominated apocryphal-pseudepigraphic. From the point of view of legends, the apocryphal books are of subordinate importance, while the pseudepigrapha are of fundamental value."[4] One can find parts of the Book of Jubilees, the Book of Jasher, and the Book of Enoch, as well as the Bible, included in Ginzberg's work.

The ***Book of Jasher*** is the most historically accurate writing of any Hebraic text found to date, but it is not considered 'inspired'. "If we are to believe the text itself, this history book was written over 3,500 years ago. It is approximately the same age as the biblical book of Genesis. It covers about the same time period as Genesis and Exodus but has about twice as much information in it than Genesis. It answers a lot of questions raised in

Genesis…the book of Jasher and several other ancient non-biblical Hebrew texts were brought from Jerusalem to Spain after the fall of Jerusalem in AD 70. One of the officers of Titus, Sidrus by name, was a believer in the God of the Hebrews. He made sure several sacred texts made it out of Jerusalem and into the Spanish city of Sevilia for safe keeping…The first translation from the Hebrew version of Jasher into English was completed in AD 1840."[5] Jasher, or as it is also called *'The Book of the Upright'* due to the fact that Jasher is not a proper name but in Hebrew means 'upright', is referenced three times in Bible; Joshua 10:13, 2 Samuel 1:18, and 2 Timothy 3:8. The 2 Timothy reference does not actually mention Jasher by name, but Paul does give the names of the magicians whom Moses went up against in the pharaoh's court, and the only place he would find their names is in the Book of Jasher. We must remember that Paul was a Pharisee before the road to Damascus encounter with Jesus, which means he would have read not only the Book of Jasher, but also both Enoch as well as other ancient texts that are Jewish in tradition. The fact that Jasher is mentioned in the Bible, there was no question to use it as a source. I would put Jasher right up there with Enoch as another book Christians should read.

The **Book of Enoch** falls into the category of pseudepigrapha, however, the majority of scholars and theologians believe it was written around the second century B.C. based on the findings of the Dead Sea Scrolls in Qumran in 1948.

> Enoch was considered inspired and authentic by certain Jewish sects of the first century B.C. and remained popular for at least five hundred years. The earliest Ethiopian text was apparently derived from a Greek manuscript of the Book of Enoch, which itself was a copy of an earlier text… the Dead Sea Scrolls found at Qumran prove the book was in existence long before the time of Jesus Christ…the first century Christians accepted the Book of Enoch as inspired, if not authentic. They relied on it to understand the origin and purpose of many things, from angels to wind, sun, and stars. In fact, many of the key concepts used by Jesus Christ himself seem directly connected to terms and ideas in the Book of Enoch. It is hard to avoid

the evidence that Jesus not only studied the book, but also respected it highly enough to allude to its doctrine and content. Enoch is replete with mentions of the coming kingdom and other holy themes. It was not only Jesus who quoted phrases or ideas from Enoch, there are over one hundred comments in the New Testament which find precedence in the Book of Enoch.[6] (Lumpkin, *Enoch*, 11–12)

Luke 9:35, in the original Greek, reads: "This is My son, the Elect One. Hear Him!" The term 'Elect One' is used by Enoch fourteen times. Jude 1:14–15 states, "Now Enoch, the seventh from Adam, prophesied about these men also, saying, 'Behold, the Lord comes with ten thousands of His saints, to execute judgment on all, to convict all who are ungodly among them of all their ungodly deeds which they have committed in an ungodly way, and of all the harsh things which ungodly sinners have spoken against Him'." Jude quotes Enoch word for word.

All of these sources have some truth in them. However, the Bible is the only absolute truth source that we have and only speaks to what happened before the flood in the first six chapters of Genesis, so I had to look elsewhere and find other ancient texts that did so. I am not taking anything away from the Bible for it is the Word of God, but some may say that I am adding to it, which I guess I am considering the fact that I am going to expound on what happened in the Bible before the flood of Noah. All of these sources were, at one time or another considered 'inspired' by the early church fathers with the exception of **The First and Second Books of Adam and Eve**, which are considered literature, albeit pretty remarkable literature to say the least.

Believe me, this book is in no way 'inspired', although I do believe that God put this on my heart for a reason and purpose, and maybe the purpose is to teach both believer and non-believer about what happened before the great flood and the reasoning for it. The only book in the Bible that we are not to take away from or add to is Revelation. One can read in Revelation 22:18–19: "For I testify to everyone who hears the words of the prophecy of this book: If anyone adds to these things, God will add to him the plagues that are written in this book; and if anyone takes away from the words of the book of this prophecy, God shall take away his part from the Book of Life, from the holy city, and from the things which are written in this book." As you read you will notice Bible references in brackets at certain points, these will be for your reading purpose to compare the two and are taken from the New King James Version. There will be direct Bible quotes at the beginning of each chapter and in certain instances I will quote the Bible to drive home a point, and these come from the New King James Version as well. The reader will notice bracketed Bible verses within the source quote itself; these are of my doing to show a parallel to the Word of God. You will also notice that the "s" in satan is not capitalized. I did not want to give him the satisfaction of being proper being that he is the most unproper being ever created.

I have basically put in order these texts in the way that I saw fit to explain, in a sense, what happened before the flood. This was an extremely hard undertaking in deciding what to put in here, as not to offend those believers who are very traditional and have never read anything outside the Bible when it comes to spiritual matters, or even history for that matter. Again, with the exception of the **Book of Jasher** and the **Book of Enoch**, thanks to the Ethiopians, these were lost to time and history until the finding of the Dead Sea Scrolls. I have prayed to God all the time about this book and whether or not to put it down, so here it is. I am going to weave these sources together and tell a story, a story of forgiveness, a story of grace and mercy, a story of justice, and a story of love that was eventually fulfilled and accomplished when Jesus Christ suffered on the cross of salvation for all of our sins. The purpose for me writing this book is to prove that Jesus was, is, and always will be the King of Kings and the Lord of Lords, the Alpha and the Omega, the beginning, and the end (Revelation 1:4–8, 11).

My love of history did not start until I was a sophomore in college. I originally went to college to get my degree in Broadcast Journalism due to my love of sports and competition, but God would show me and tell me that history is much better, and it is. I received my degree in History from a little-known university just south of Atlanta, GA called Clayton State University. The good thing about Clayton State is that the Georgia Archives and the Southeast Division of the National Archives is located practically on the campus itself and I was able to spend time in both places while getting my degree.

I am a sinner like everyone else in this world, but am blessed to have His forgiveness, grace, and mercy, but more importantly His love that was shown through His son Jesus Christ on the cross of salvation at Golgotha. I have never used my degree in history in my professional life until now with the writing of this book. But this life is not about financial gain or fame; it is about your relationship with God and discipleship. I have truly become a disciple of Jesus Christ through the learning of history and everything that has happened since Adam and Eve were kicked out of the Garden of Eden. The hands of God are on all of history, hence the name HiStory (ha ha). A perfect example of this is sometimes referred to as 'The Silent Years', when Israel did not have any prophets speaking on behalf of God (end of the Babylonian captivity until the birth of Jesus). However, if you know anything about what happened during this period in history then you know that Alexander 'The Great' was conquering the known world at this exact same time and making Greek the official language; God was working in the secular world. He would use the Apostle Paul and the others of course, to spread the Good News of Jesus Christ through the Gentile nations using the Greek language.

I have always been fascinated with what happened before the great flood of Noah because there are only a few chapters dedicated to it in the Bible and also due to when Jesus says in Matthew 24:36–39: "But of that day and hour no one knows, not even the angels of heaven, but My Father only. But as the days of Noah were, so also will the coming of the Son of Man be. For as in the days before the flood, they were eating and drinking, marrying and giving in marriage, until the day that Noah entered the ark, and did not know until the flood came and took them all away, so also will the coming of the Son of Man be" [Luke 17:26–27]. So, we may not know when the Savior will be coming back for His Church, but we can know what happened before and during the 'days of Noah' by reading other books, not included in our canonized scripture, that discuss what happened and the reason for the great flood.

Have you ever looked at the megalithic structures from around the world and wondered how they were built or by whom? From Puma Punku in Bolivia to Carahunge in present-day Armenia, from Egypt to the Mayan civilization in Central America, from Stonehenge in England to Gobekli Tepe in Turkey, from Easter Island to Nan Madol in Micronesia, from the Carnac stones in France to the Temple of Baalbek in Lebanon, and many others. You can see that off the coast of India and Japan that there were ancient cities that are now below sea level thanks to the great flood. All of these ancient sites are built with cut and hewn stones, whether granite or basalt, that weigh anywhere from ten to hundreds of tons per stone. And they are built in similar fashion telling me that they learned from somebody and somewhere. With our building technology today, we cannot replicate these structures. There are pyramids all over this earth, in every corner and land. Now, not all of these cities were built before the great flood, but it is my belief that some of them were. How did these ancient peoples build such gigantic structures? Not only that, but how did they get these huge stones in position and how did they traverse these stones over rugged territory, in some cases hundreds of miles? Where did they learn to build? One cannot really know the truth of the matter as it pertains to these huge ancient megalithic structures but using ancient texts one can ascertain as to the possibility that these technologically advanced civilizations, who were said to be hunters and gatherers from mainstream archaeology, learned from the fallen angels and had the help of their giant offspring.

What you will find in this book is the hardships that Adam and Eve faced out of the Garden of Eden thanks to satan. You will find the fall of satan and his hosts and also his aspirations when it comes to us, the seed of Adam and, eventually Noah. You will read about the fallen angels and what they taught humans, and you will read about their giant children who corrupted the earth. You will see that Jesus has always been and will be the King of kings and Lord of lords. You will read about a man named Enoch, who was the first prophet, who never died an earthly death (neither did the prophet Elijah – see 2 Kings 2), and who saw Jesus in the heavens before creation and on this earth in the last days. You will read about Noah and the reasoning behind God flooding the earth. And finally, you will read about Jesus and the prophecies about him told to Adam about His future sacrifice and revealed to Enoch by God Himself about His future judgment and coming kingdom.

Now, I know that not everybody who is going to read this book is a

Christian or a believer in the God of Abraham, Isaac, and Jacob. If you do not have a relationship with God through His son Jesus, it is my hope and prayer that this book in some form or fashion can help with that. But please, start with the Bible as the infallible Word of God. Why the Bible? "It is because the Bible is true and trusted and valued by so many people that so many manuscripts survive from it; It is because the Bible is authored by one unchanging God with one purpose that consistency can be found among so many books written over such a long period of time by so many diverse writers; It is because the Bible is written by a caring God with all knowledge that its laws were so wholesome ahead of their time; It is because the Bible is authored by an all-knowing, truthful, faithful God that it is so full of fulfilled prophecy; It is because the Bible is true that its archaeological claims are so dependable; It is because the Bible is preserved by an all-powerful, just, unchanging God that manuscripts separated by multiple centuries are so similar."[7] This work just expands on what happened before the great flood of Noah using other ancient Hebraic texts.

Now that you know where I am coming from with the sources that I chose to use, let us get started. I hope you enjoy the ride!

In His Grace,

Paul Jared Arnold

Introduction

Yes, there was a world-wide flood! The Bible points to it. Genesis 6:7 says, "So the Lord said, 'I will destroy man whom I have created from the face of the earth, both man and beast, creeping things and birds of the air, for I am sorry that I have made them'." Genesis 6:13 states, "And God said to Noah, 'The end of all flesh has come before Me, for the earth is filled with violence through them; and behold, I will destroy them with the earth'." Again, we find that Genesis 7:19–24 states, "And the waters prevailed exceedingly on the earth, and all the high hills under the whole heaven were covered. The waters prevailed fifteen cubits (22.5 feet) upward, and the mountains were covered. And all flesh died that moved on the earth: birds and cattle and beasts and every creeping thing that creeps on the earth, and every man. All in whose nostrils was the breath of the spirit of life, all that was on the dry land, died. So He destroyed all living things which were on the face of the ground: both man and cattle, creeping thing and bird of the air. They were destroyed from the earth. Only Noah and those who were with him in the ark remained alive. And the waters prevailed on the earth one hundred and fifty days." And finally, Jesus says in Luke 17:26–27, "And as it was in the days of Noah, so it will be also in the days of the Son of Man: They ate, they drank, they married wives, they were given in marriage, until the day that Noah entered the ark, and the flood came and destroyed them all."

Yes, there was a world-wide flood! History points to it. As noted in the Preface, history is the study of written documents that were passed down orally until someone with the ability to write down the stories does so. There are flood stories from every corner of the earth. "As the fact of a global flood was passed down through history, children and grandchildren of survivors would modify what they had due to imperfect memories…

but the basic ideas would remain the same."[1] In the Americas there are the Ojibwe peoples with their hero being Waynaboozhoo, the Algonquin with their hero being Manabozho, the Cree and their hero Wisagatcak, and the Inca peoples and their hero known as Unu Pachakati. In Europe there are the Greeks with their hero being Deucalion and the Norse with their hero being Bergelmir. And in Asia there are the peoples of India with their hero being named Manu, the Akkadian empire has the story of Atrahasis, and, of course, the *Epic of Gilgamesh* from Mesopotamia. And "…the survivors of the global flood passed on to their children first-hand accounts. Yes, we would expect the accounts to be degraded in accuracy, and some more-so than others. Be that as it may, human memory points to a global flood."[2] Also, the Chinese have a flood account with their hero being named Nuwa, and it is also a historical fact that the Chinese are considered to have had the first known writing system. However, other cultures developed writing systems around the same time in the form of hieroglyphs of the Egyptian civilization and cuneiform of the Sumerian/ Mesopotamian civilization. "One complex Chinese pictogram (actually an ideogram, because it expresses a complex thought) describes a time of great flooding, a time when a boat was used to rescue eight people. This supports the Biblical account of Noah and his family."[3] When you say the Chinese hero's name of Nuwa, aren't you saying Noah?

Yes, there was a world-wide flood! Science points to it. Geology, as defined by Merriam-Webster, is a science that deals with the history of the earth and its life especially as recorded in rocks. "When applied to geological formations supposed to have taken hundreds of millions of years to form experimental data and paleohydraulic analysis set the duration of their formation at a maximum of several weeks. The geological time scale and dating of the fossil record have thus been invalidated by observation tested by meticulous laboratory experiments."[4] Even "…'evolutionists' agree with creation scientists that the cutting of the Grand Canyon happened rapidly – not by way of millions of years."[5] What about the dinosaur (big lizard-like creature) footprints found all over the world in the layers of rocks? "Andrew Snelling, a PhD geologist from the University of Sydney, wrote: 'Flood geologists have a satisfying explanation for fossilized dinosaur footprints in dolomite layers. But conventional geologists, who insist on slow-and-gradual geologic processes, struggle to explain both the dolomite layers and the preservation of the dinosaur footprints'."[6] And anyone who has laid or poured cement knows that it hardens in just a few hours so the "tracks were preserved because the animals were not just walking in mud but in flood sediment mud that retains impressions while hardening…This cannot be just an ordinary flood; it made rock."[7]

Yes, there was a world-wide flood! The rapid burial of creatures points to it as well as the pattern of burial, meaning the heavier creatures and those unable to swim or fly would be buried first. "The fossil remains of once-living creatures, wherever they are found in the rocks of the earth, should show a logical order of superposition, a tendency for organisms of heavier specific weights, simpler structure, of lower-elevation habitats, and lesser capability for swimming, running, or flying, to be entrapped earlier and buried deeper in the deluge sediments. More complex organisms in upper level habitats would be buried later and higher…deposition pattern is found in the geologic record all over the earth."[8] Even "fish are found frozen in sediment swallowing other fish…an ichthyosaur was buried and fossilized while giving birth…These remarkable preservations reveal sudden death with little time for flesh to decay."[9] Every creature that lived on earth, dry land, died in the days of the world-wide flood [Genesis 7:22 and Luke 17:27]. "Stefan Anitei, a Science Editor, wrote in 'Death Pose in Dinosaurs: Brain Damage, Not Drying Muscles – The Opisthotonous': 'Fossilized dinosaurs can be found in the most bizarre postures, like mouth wide-open, head thrown back and recurved tail…The classical explanation was that the dinosaurs died in water and the currents positioned the bones that way…Now, researchers say that the contorted position is a result of agonized death throes typical of brain damage and asphyxiation'…animals caught in a global flood would be asphyxiated…it would have to be a quick death, as the death pose relaxes in a few days."[10]

Yes, there was a world-wide flood! "The preponderance of fossils all over the earth and high above sea level, however, points to a worldwide cataclysmic event."[11] You can find the fossils of sea creatures in the Andes Mountains, the Rocky Mountains, and the Himalayan Mountains. Not only is the Bible accurate and true, but "the scientific implications of a global flood support the Biblical account rather than a sequence of local floods. The waters for a global flood could only have come from great upheavals of the oceanic basins, the foundations of the deep, or from an atmospheric source other than the vapor content of the current atmosphere."[12]

Yes, there was a world-wide flood! Again, the Bible points to it. Psalm 104:5–9 states, "You who laid the foundations of the earth, so that it should not be moved forever, You covered it with the deep as with a garment; the waters stood above the mountains. At Your rebuke they fled; at the voice of Your thunder they hastened away. They went up over the mountains; they went down into the valleys, to the place which You founded for them. You have set a boundary that they may not pass over, that they may not return to cover the earth." And 2 Peter 3:1–7 says, "Beloved, I now write to you this second epistle (in both of which I stir up your pure minds by way of reminder), that you may be mindful of the words which were spoken before by the holy prophets, and of the commandment of us, the apostles of the Lord and Savior, knowing this first: that scoffers will come in the last days, walking according to their own lusts, and saying, 'Where is the promise of His coming? For since the fathers fell asleep, all things continue as they were from the beginning of creation.' For this they willfully forget: that by the Word of God the heavens were of old, and the earth standing out of water and in the water, by which the world that then existed perished, being flooded with water. But the heavens and the earth which are now preserved by the same Word, are reserved for fire until the day of judgment and perdition of ungodly men."

Creation & the Fall

"In the beginning God created the heavens and the earth." [Genesis 1:1]

"For since the creation of the world His invisible attributes are clearly seen, being understood by the things that are made, even His eternal power and Godhead..." [Romans 1:20]

"But from the beginning of the creation, God 'made them male and female'." [Mark 10:6]

"Therefore the Lord God sent him out of the garden of Eden to till the ground from which he was taken. So He drove out the man..." [Genesis 3:23–24]

"For in six days the Lord made the heavens and the earth, the sea, and all that is in them, and rested the seventh day..." [Exodus 20:11]

There are creation myths, or stories, from every religion and culture on earth. There is the Norse creation myth found in the *Eddic* poetry written around the 13th Century AD, but probably dates to the BC era. It describes a giant called Ymir and how Odin and his brothers killed him and turned his flesh and bones into earth, seas, and the heavens. It also mentions a tree called Yggdrasill (World tree, Steed of Ygg, or Odin, which means 'terrible one') that connects the nine worlds (Niflheim, Muspelheim, Asgard, Vanaheim, Jotunheim, Midgard (earth), Alfheim, Svartalfheim, and Nidavellir) with nine roots.[1] There is the Sumerian/Babylonian creation myth found in the *Enuma Elish* (aka 'The Seven Tablets of Creation') that dates back to the second millennium BC. It describes how Apsu (fresh water) and Tiamat (salt water) give birth to Enki and his siblings and how Enki kills Apsu. It also mentions Marduk and how he kills Tiamat, and her eyes create the Tigris and Euphrates Rivers, and her flesh creates the heavens and earth. Marduk then creates humans to be servants and slaves to the gods.[2] In fact, the Sumerians and the native peoples of the Americas have a lot in common with their creation stories (the natives of both Americas were originally from that area, ever heard of the Tower of Babel) . There is the Greek myth found in *Theogony* by Hesiod and written around the 8th Century BC. There is the Japanese myth found in the *Nihon Shoki* and *Kojiki*, both were written around the 8th Century AD. There is the Hindu tale based off the *Upanishad* texts of the 7th Century BC and written in the *Mahabharata* between the 5th and 3rd Centuries BC. There are several myths about creation from the peoples of Africa and from the peoples of all the Americas. One can find creation myths everywhere and the one common theme among them all is that there was nothing in the beginning (i.e. a great chasm, or chaos, the deep, waters, a void, etc.). The term "mythology" comes from the Greek *mythos* meaning story of the people, and *logos* meaning word or speech. In essence these stories are passed down orally until someone writes it down, and information can get lost over time. Have you ever played the game telephone?

However, I believe the true account of creation can be found in the book of Genesis in the Bible. It was given directly to Moses from God Himself. There was only one eyewitness to creation:

God was it: He existed at the beginning of time [John 1:1–2]. Actually, He and only He existed before the beginning of time – before the beginning of everything that had a beginning [Colossians 1:17]; unlike humans and other created beings, God is present everywhere in the universe. He is not constrained by space [Proverbs 15:3, Jeremiah 21:24]; He is the Creator of all things [John 1:1–3, Colossians 1:16]. Therefore, He had direct experience of every aspect of every beginning; Since God is eternal [Psalm 9:7, 1 Timothy 1:17] and unchanging [Malachi 3:6, Hebrews 13:8], He has been in existence throughout the entire history of the universe for all subsequent events; God is sustainer of everything [Colossians 1:17, Hebrews 1:3], therefore He had direct experience and all knowledge of every event in the history of the universe; God's wisdom is without limit, and His understanding is complete [Psalm 147:5, 1 John 3:20]. He accurately observes, understands, and remembers all aspects of all events; Since God is unfallen and in fact instituted the curse on the creation, He is outside the effects of the Fall. Since He is truth and is uncompromised by sin, God is not only the sole eyewitness of the past, but He is also the only fully reliable witness.[3] (Wise, *Faith, Form & Time*, 5)

The Physical

You may be asking, 'Why study the physical world that God created?'

The physical world exists (so God can show Himself through it); the physical world has a reliable structure and order (so man can infer from this structure and order the nature of an unchanging God); the structure and order of the physical world is understandable by humans (so man can see God in the creation); knowledge can be gleaned from the study of the physical world (for example, the knowledge that God created it); knowledge should be gleaned from the study of the physical world (God wishes for us to know Him); physical world patterns should remain constant through time (so the same unchanging God is seen by all people regardless of when they lived); physical world patterns should remain constant through space (so the same unchanging God is seen by all people regardless of where they happened to be located); physical world patterns should be discernable in the course of a single human lifetime (so individuals can come to know Him); human senses and reason are reliable enough to discern truth about the physical world (so people can reliably infer the nature of the Creator from the physical world); human language is capable of describing, understanding, and teaching the truths about the physical world (so the Word can be known by man and information about Him can be passed on to others); truths about unseen things can be inferred from the study of observable things (so we can infer the nature of God from things that are made); physical world patterns are likely to be connected in consistent and simple ways (to point to a single Creator); observable things have causes (so that among other things, we infer the ultimate cause – God – to those things that are seen).[4] (Wise, *Faith, Form & Time*, 34–35)

You need to look at, and study, the physical world of the Creator to understand the Creator. He has order and structure and so it stands to reason that His creation would have the same. "And God formed man from the ground, and He blew into his nostrils the breath of life [Genesis 2:7], and man became a living soul endowed with speech."[5]

Let us dive deeper into what was physically created by the Hand of God:

For on the first day He created the heavens which are above and the earth [Genesis 1:1] and the waters and all the spirits which serve before Him – the angels of the presence, and the angels of sanctification, and the angels of the spirit of fire and the angels of the spirit of the winds [Revelation 7:1], and the angels of the spirit of the clouds, and of darkness, and of snow and of hail and of hoar frost, and the angels of the voices and of the thunder and of the lightning [Revelation 4:5, 11:19, 16:18], and the angels of the spirits of cold and of heat, and of winter and of spring and of autumn and of summer, and of all the spirits of His creatures which are in the heavens and on the earth, He created the abysses and the darkness, eventide and night, and the light, dawn and day [Genesis 1:3–5], which He hath prepared in the knowledge of His heart. And thereupon we saw His works, and praised Him, and lauded before Him on account of all His works [Genesis 1:1–5] … And on the second day He created the firmament in the midst of the waters, and the waters were divided on that day – half of them went up above and half of them went down below the firmament that was in the midst over the face of the whole earth [Genesis 1:6–8]... And on the third day He commanded the waters to pass from off the face of the whole earth into one place, and the dry land to appear [Genesis 1:9]. And the waters did so as He commanded them, and they retired from off the face of the earth into one place outside of this firmament, and the dry land appeared. And on that day He created for them all the seas according to their separate gathering-places, and all the rivers, and the gatherings of the waters in the mountains and on all the earth, and all the lakes, and all the dew of the earth, and the seed which is sown, and all sprouting things, and fruit-bearing trees [Genesis 1:11–12], and trees of the wood, and the Garden of Eden, in Eden, and all plants after their kind...And on the fourth day He created the sun and the moon and the stars, and set them in the firmament of the heaven, to give light upon all the earth, and to rule over the day and the night, and divide the light from darkness [Genesis 1:14–19]...

And on the fifth day He created great sea monsters in the depths of the waters, for these were the first things of flesh that were created by His hands, the fish and everything that moves in the waters, and everything that flies, the birds and all their kind [Genesis 1:20–23]…And on the sixth day He created all the animals of the earth, and all cattle, and everything that moves on the earth [Genesis 1:24–25]. And after all this He created man, a man and a woman created He them, and gave him dominion over all that is upon the earth, and in the seas, and over everything that flies, and over beasts and over cattle, and over everything that moves on the earth, and over the whole earth, and over all this He gave him dominion [Genesis 1:26–28]…And He finished all His work on the sixth day – all that is in the heavens and on the earth, and in the seas and in the abysses, and in the light and in the darkness, and in everything [Genesis 2:1]…[6] (Johnson, *Jubilees*, 15–17)

Notice the order of the Creator God. He did not bring forth man until everything else was created that the man would need to sustain him.

In the Genesis account the author, in chapter two, takes a closer look at the creation of Adam and Eve, and here is one account that goes deeper into day three:

On the third day, God planted the garden in the east of the earth [Genesis 2:8], on the border of the world in the eastward direction toward and beyond the rising sun. There one finds nothing but water that encompasses the whole world and reaches to the borders of heaven. And to the north of the garden there is a sea of water, clear and pure to the taste, unlike anything else; so that, through the clearness one may look into the depths of the earth. And when a man washes himself in it, he becomes perfectly clean and perfectly white, even if he were dark. And God created that sea of His own good pleasure,

> for He knew what would come of the man He would make; so that after he had left the garden, because of his transgression, men should be born in the earth. Among them are righteous ones who will die, whose souls God would raise at the last day when all of them will return to their flesh, bathe in the water of that sea, and repent of their sins.[7] (Lumpkin, *Adam & Eve*, 8)

Now this is remarkably interesting because God did plant the Garden of Eden in the east and He, through Jesus, is going to raise the dead at the end and all believers will be washed of their sins.

Everything created gives praise to their Creator [Revelation 5:13]. Psalm 19:1–6 states, "The heavens declare the glory of God; and the firmament shows His handiwork. Day unto day utters speech, and night unto night reveals knowledge. There is no speech nor language where their voice is not heard. Their line has gone out through all the earth, and their words to the end of the world. In them He has set a tabernacle for the sun, which is like a bridegroom coming out of his chamber, and rejoices like a strong man to run its race. Its rising is from one end of heaven, and its circuit to the other end; and there is nothing hidden from its heat." The birds sing in the morning, the beasts of the field speak in their own language, the lights in the sky proclaim His holiness, the trees and plants obey the commands of God, and even the rocks cry out. Why do certain animals migrate at their exact time? It is because of their Creator. A couple examples of this are when some birds fly south to get away from the cold months and when bears know exactly when to begin preparation for their hibernation. "The whole of creation was called into existence by God unto His glory, and each creature has its own hymn of praise wherewith to extol the Creator. Heaven and earth, Paradise and hell, desert and field, rivers and seas – all have their own way of paying homage to God. The hymn of the earth is, 'From the uttermost part of the earth have we heard songs, glory to the Righteous'. The sea exclaims, 'Above the voices of many waters, the mighty breakers of the sea, the Lord on high is mighty' [Psalm 95:3–5]. Also the celestial bodies and the elements proclaim the praise of their Creator [Psalm 19:1–4] – the sun, moon, and stars, the clouds and the winds, lightning and dew."[8] Not only these, but we also were created to give glory and honor and praise to the One who created us. We were created for relationship with Him, hence the fact that He walked and conversed with Adam in the Garden of Eden [Genesis 2:16–18 and Genesis 3:8–13]. We are to worship the Creator, not creation.

God created everything in six days and on the seventh He rested [Genesis 2:2]. This was done on purpose to show man how he was to work and notice how God did not create man until everything else was made. This too was done on purpose as everything had to be ready for the man who was to come and have dominion over the creation.

> The world was made for man, though he was the last comer among its creatures. This was design. He was to find all things ready for him…At the same time man's late appearance on earth is to convey an admonition to humility [1 Peter 5:5]. Let him be aware of being proud [Psalm 138:6 and Isaiah 2:12], lest he invite the retort that the gnat is older than he. The superiority of man to the other creatures is apparent in the very manner of his creation…The hair upon his head corresponds to the woods of the earth, his tears to a river, his mouth to the ocean. Also, the world resembles the ball of his eye: the ocean that encircles the earth is like unto the white of the eye, the dry land is the iris, Jerusalem is the pupil [Zechariah 2:8], and the Temple the image mirrored in the eye…He unites both heavenly and earthly qualities within himself. In four he resembles the angels, in four the beasts. His power of speech, his discriminating intellect, his upright walk, the glance of his eye – they all make an angel of him. But, on the other hand, he eats and drinks, secretes the waste matter in his body, propagates his kind, and dies, like the beast of the field. Therefore God said before the creation of man: 'The celestials are not propagated, but they are immortal; the beings on earth are propagated, but they die. I will create man to be the union of the two, so that when he sins, when he behaves like a beast, death shall overtake him [Genesis 2:16]; but

if he refrains from sin, he shall live forever'.[9] (Ginzberg, *Legends*, 21)

Humans are superior to every other creature on earth in that we can reason within our minds. We automatically know what is good and what is bad. This was instilled in our hearts at creation in that we were made in the image of God [Genesis 1:26–27]. A beast of the field, lion or tiger or any carnivorous wild animal, does not have reason within them, they see prey and they go kill and eat. We, however, know that it is evil to murder or steal or cheat. We are not to be proud according to King Solomon [Proverbs 8:13, 11:2, 16:5] and are to be humble [James 4:10] in all aspects of life, lest we fall [Proverbs 16:18–19]. And we do fall all the time, but thanks to God for His grace and mercy, and our ability to ask for forgiveness.

Men and women have all of the same qualities and they look alike in physical form with some noticeable differences. "…Adam came from the hands of the Creator fully and completely developed. He was not like a child, but like a man of twenty years of age. The dimensions of his body were gigantic, reaching from heaven to earth, or, what amounts to the same, from east to west. Among later generations of men, there but few who in a measure resembled Adam in his extraordinary size and physical perfections. Samson possessed his strength [Judges 14:6, 15:15–16, 16:23–30], Saul his neck [1 Samuel 9:2], Absalom his hair [2 Samuel 14:26], Asahel his fleetness of foot [2 Samuel 2:18], Uzziah his forehead, Josiah his nostrils, Zedekiah his eyes, and Zerubbabel his voice…His spiritual qualities kept pace with his personal charm, for God had fashioned his soul with particular care. She is the image of God, and as God fills the world, so the soul fills the human body; as God sees all things, and is seen by none, so the soul sees, but cannot be seen; as God guides the world, so the soul guides the body; as God in His holiness is pure, so is the soul; and as God dwells in secret, so doth the soul."[10] Adam was created perfect in his physical form. I believe that is why Paul calls Jesus the last Adam [1 Corinthians 15:45]. Adam was made perfect and Jesus lived a perfect life [1 Corinthians 15:20–23], however there are other reasons I believe Paul called Jesus the last Adam and I will get into that later on. "The physical formation of woman is far more complicated than that of man, as it must be for the function of child-bearing, and likewise the intelligence of woman matures more quickly than the intelligence of man. Many of the physical and psychical differences between the two sexes must be attributed to the fact that man was formed from the ground and woman from bone...The man must ask the woman to be his wife, and not the woman the man to be her husband, because it is man who sustained the loss of his rib, and he sallies forth to make good his loss again. The very differences between the sexes in garb and social forms go back to the origin of man and woman for their reasons."[11] However, after Adam saw and named all the animals God saw that there was none like him so He made the man sleep so He could create his like out of him, hence the name 'wo-man'.

Israel, the Hebrews, through the seed of Abraham has always held precedence in the eyes of God, even before creation. "It was...Israel who was taken into special consideration at the time man was made. All other creatures were instructed to change their nature, if Israel should ever need their help in the course of His history. The sea was ordered to divide before Moses [Exodus 14:13–31], and the heavens to give ear to the words of the leader; the sun and the moon were bidden to stand still [Joshua 10:12–14], the ravens to feed Elijah [1 Kings 2:2–4], the fire to spare the three youths in the furnace [Daniel 3:19–25], the lion to do no harm to Daniel, the fish to spew forth Jonah [Jonah 2:10], and the heavens to open before Ezekiel."[12] Isn't it interesting that God would stop the sun and the moon from moving, and yet we are told by 'Science' and every so-called space agency in the world that the earth is the one that moves?

The Naming & The Two Beasts

All creatures that live on the dry land, earth, got their names from Adam when God brought them to him. Here are a couple of accounts of what took place: "Listen to me, my children, today. In those days when the Lord came down to earth for Adam's sake, and visited all His creatures, which He created Himself, after all these He created Adam, and the Lord called all the beasts of the earth, all the reptiles, and all the birds that soar in the air, and brought them all before the face of our father Adam. And Adam gave names to all things living on the earth [Genesis 2:19–20]. And the Lord appointed him ruler over all, and subjected all things to him under his hands, and made them dumb and made them dull that they would be commanded by man, and be in subjection and obedience to him [Genesis 1:26–30]."[13] "…God assembled the whole world of animals before him…Adam…spoke without hesitation: 'O Lord of the world! The proper name for this animal is ox, for this one horse, for this one lion, for this one camel'. And so he called all in turn by name, suiting the name to the peculiarity of the animal. Then God asked him what his name was to be, and he said Adam, because he had been created out of Adamah, dust of the earth. Again, God asked him His own name, and he said: 'Adonai, Lord, because Thou art Lord over all creatures' – the very name God had given unto Himself, the name by which the angels call Him, the name that will remain immutable evermore. But without the gift of the Holy Spirit, Adam could not have found names for all…"[14] Adam even gave a name to his Creator and he could not have done that without the spirit of God upon him. We have access to that Holy Spirit today [John 14:16–17, 26 and Acts 1:4–8] thanks to the sacrifice Jesus made on our behalf. Before Jesus only a certain few had access to that spirit and they are known as the prophets (Isaiah, Jeremiah, Ezekiel, Daniel, Elijah, and others, as well as those that form the last twelve books of the Old Testament known as the 'minor prophets').

There are also two huge beasts, one in the seas and the other on the earth, that were created at the respective times the sea and land animals were created. The sea creature is named Leviathan and the land creature is called Behemoth, and you can read about both of these in the Old Testament book of Job.

Leviathan: "And on that day two monsters were separated from one another…Leviathan, to dwell in the abyss of the ocean over the fountains of the waters…Behemoth, who occupied with his breast a wasted wilderness named Duidain, on the east of the garden where the elect and the righteous dwell…And I asked the other angel to show me the might of those monsters, how they were separated on one day and thrown, the one into the abyss of the sea, and the other to the earth's desert…And the angel of Peace who was with me, said to me: 'These two monsters, prepared in accordance with the greatness of the Lord, will feed them the punishment of the Lord'"[15] [Job 40:15 – 41:34].

Behemoth: "Behemot(h) matches Leviathan in strength…He is so monstrous that he requires the produce of a thousand mountains for his daily food. All the water that flows through the bed of the Jordan in a year suffices him exactly for one gulp. It therefore was necessary to give him one stream entirely for his own use, a stream flowing forth from Paradise, called Yubal. Behemot(h), too, is destined to be served to the pious as an appetizing dainty, but before they enjoy his flesh, they will be permitted to view the mortal combat between Leviathan and Behemot(h)…"[16] [Job 40:15–24].

> The ruler over the sea-animals is Leviathan…So enormous is Leviathan that to quench his thirst he needs all the water that flows from the Jordan into the sea. His food consists of the fish which go between his jaws of their own accord. When he is hungry, a hot breath blows from his nostrils, and it makes the waters of the great sea seething hot. Formidable though Behemot(h), the other monster, is, he feels insecure until he is certain the Leviathan has satisfied his thirst…But Leviathan is more than merely large and strong; he is wonderfully made besides. His fins radiate brilliant light, the very sun is obscured by it, and also his eyes shed such splendor that frequently the sea is illuminated suddenly by it. No wonder that this marvelous beast is the plaything of God, in whom He takes His pastime [Job 41:1–34]…The real purpose of Leviathan is to be served up as dainty to the pious in the world to come…When his last hour arrives, God will summon the angels to enter into combat with the monster. But no sooner will Leviathan cast his glance at them than they will flee in fear and dismay from the field of battle. They will return to the charge with swords, but in vain, for his scales can turn back steel like straw. They will be equally unsuccessful when they attempt to kill him with by throwing darts and slinging stones; such missiles will rebound without leaving the least impression on his body. Disheartened, the angels will give up the combat, and God will command Leviathan and Behemot(h) to enter into a

duel with each other. The issue will be that both will drop dead, Behemot(h) slaughtered by a blow of Leviathan's fins, and Leviathan killed by a lash of Behemot(h)'s tail.[17] (Ginzberg, *Legends*, 14–15)

It has been said that Behemoth is a hippopotamus, but that is highly unlikely given the size and shear power of this beast. Maybe Behemoth is a huge alligator or crocodile, who knows what this is, but I have always thought that there was at least something excessively big that lives in the seas other than a big shark or whale, and that is Leviathan. I believe Leviathan is in fact a dragon, but it lives in the ocean, in the deep or abysses, and all sea creatures know of it and are afraid.

One interesting point about these two beasts is that the angels themselves cannot kill them and are afraid of them. They have to kill each other, and they do it in front of the world, a sort of King Kong vs. Goliath battle in real life. We, as believers in Jesus, are invited to take part in the 'marriage supper of the Lamb' [Revelation 19:6–9]. Could the flesh of these two beasts be our food? According to these texts they are, and it makes perfect sense that they should be prepared for Jesus and his wedding to the Church.

The Fall & The Curses

When Adam and Eve sinned in the Garden of Eden it affected everything that God created from the animals to the plants and from the lights in the sky to the earth itself. Man was not originally intended to work as hard as we do for the bare necessities to live. Man was also not intended to hunt animals for food because all that was needed was in the Garden of Eden. I believe that all creatures were herbivores, plant eaters [Genesis 1:29–30]. But everything would change when sin entered the world.

Paradise being such as it was, it was, naturally, not necessary for Adam to work the land. True, the Lord God put the man into the Garden of Eden to dress it and to keep it [Genesis 2:8, 15]…Adam was to eat only the green things of the field. But the prohibition against the use of animals for food was revoked in Noah's time, after the deluge. Nevertheless, Adam was not cut off from the enjoyment of meat dishes. Though he was not permitted to slaughter animals for the appeasing of his appetite, the angels brought him meat and wine, serving him like attendants. And as the angels ministered to his wants, so also the animals. They were wholly under his dominion, and their food they took out of his hand and out of Eve's. In all respects, the animal world had a different relation to Adam from their relation to his descendants. Not only did they know the language of man, but they respected the image of God, and they feared the first human couple, all of which changed into the opposite after the fall of man.[18] (Ginzberg, *Legends*, 28)

I passionately believe that every animal, not just the serpent, talked to Adam and Eve. How else could they have had dominion over them? "And on that day was closed the mouth of all beasts, and of cattle, and of birds, and of whatever walks, and of whatever moves, so that they could no longer speak: for they had all spoken one with another with one lip and with one tongue."[19]

We just read how the animal world was affected due to their sin, but now we will read about the physical curses upon mankind and God's other creations.

When Adam and Eve heard God approaching, they hid among the trees [Genesis 3:8] – which would not have been possible before the fall. Before he committed his trespass, Adam's height was from the heavens to the earth, but afterward it was reduced to one hundred ells (150 feet). Another consequence of his sin was the fear Adam felt when he heard the voice of God [Genesis 3:10]: before his fall it had not disquieted him in the least...Standing at the gate of Paradise, He but asked, 'Where art thou, Adam?' Thus did God desire to teach man a rule of polite behavior, never to enter the house of another without announcing himself...They were intended to bring home to Adam the vast difference between his latter and his former state – between his supernatural size then and his shrunken size now; between the lordship of God over him then and the lordship of the serpent over him now.[20] (Ginzberg, *Legends*, 30)

Now, was mankind really that big? It is my belief that everything was bigger before the flood of Noah (trees, plants, animals, and yes, humans). It is hard for us to imagine human beings that big, but there were 'giants in those days' [Genesis 6:4], however, the giants after the flood (i.e. Goliath and his brothers, and the people living in the land the Israelites were to take, Canaan) were born of human men and women whereas the giants before the flood were born from the fallen angels and human women. I will get into a little of that in the chapter on Enoch. Have you ever seen the fossil remains of those animals (i.e. the woolly mammoth, the saber tooth tiger, and yes, dinosaurs or big reptiles/lizards)?

Not only did mankind lose their natural state in form, but they also were cursed to live on this earth and face all kinds of trouble that they knew not before their sin. Now, we know one of the curses towards the woman was pain in childbirth [Genesis 3:16], but God apparently gave ten curses to mankind, the serpent, and the earth. Here are the curses for mankind: "...also the punishment of Adam was tenfold: he lost his celestial clothing – God stripped it off him; in sorrow he was to earn his daily bread [Genesis 3:17]; the food he ate was to be turned from good into bad; his children were to wander from land to land; his body was to exude sweat [Genesis 3:19]; he was to have an evil inclination; in death his body was to be prey of the worms; animals were to have power over him, in that they could slay him; his days were to be few and full of trouble; in the end he was to render account of all his doings on earth."[21]

Here are the curses for the serpent:

God inflicted the curse upon the serpent without hearing his defense; for the serpent is a villain, and the wicked are good debaters...Therefore did God not enter into an argument with the serpent, but straightway decreed the following ten punishments: the mouth of the serpent was closed, and his power of speech taken away; his hands and feet were hacked off [Genesis 3:14]; the earth was given him as food [Genesis 3:14]; he must suffer great pain in sloughing his skin; enmity is to exist between him and man [Genesis 3:15]; if he eats the choicest viands, or drinks the sweetest beverages, they all change into dust in his mouth [Genesis 3:14]; the pregnancy of the female serpent lasts seven years; men shall seek to kill him as soon as they catch sight of him; even in the future world, where all beings will be blessed, he will not escape the punishment decreed for him [Revelation 20:1–3, 10]; he will vanish from out of the Holy Land if Israel walks in the ways of God. Furthermore, God spake to the serpent: 'I created thee to be king over all animals, cattle and the beasts of the field alike; but thou wast not satisfied. Therefore thou shalt be cursed above all cattle and above every beast of the field. I created thee of upright posture; but thou wast not satisfied. Therefore thou shalt go upon thy belly. I created thee to eat the same food as man; but thou wast not satisfied. Therefore thou shalt eat dust all the days of thy life. Thou didst seek to cause the death of Adam in order to espouse his wife. Therefore I will put enmity between thee and the woman' [Genesis 3:14–15].[22] (Ginzberg, *Legends*, 30)

And finally, the curses for the earth and the celestial lights, although this account says that only curses fell on the earth and moon:

The earth fared no better…the earth did not do its whole duty in connection with the sin of Adam. God had appointed the sun and the earth witnesses to testify against Adam in case he committed a trespass. The sun, accordingly, had grown dark the instant Adam became guilty of disobedience, but the earth, not knowing how to take notice of Adam's fall, disregarded it altogether. The earth also had to suffer a tenfold punishment: independent before, she was hereafter to wait to be watered by the rain from above; sometimes the fruits of the earth fail; the grain she brings forth is stricken with blasting and mildew; she must produce all sorts of noxious vermin; thenceforth she was to be divided into valleys and mountains; she must grow barren trees, bearing no fruit; thorns and thistles sprout from her [Genesis 3:18]; much is sown in the earth, but little is harvested; in time to come the earth will have to disclose her blood, and shall no more cover her slain; and, finally, she shall, one day, 'wax old like a garment'… The earth is not the only thing created that was made to suffer through the sin of Adam. The same fate overtook the moon. When the serpent seduced Adam and Eve [Genesis 3:1–7], and exposed their nakedness, they wept bitterly, and with them wept the heavens, and the sun and the stars, and all created beings and things up to the throne of God. The very angels and the celestial beings were grieved by the transgression of Adam. The moon alone laughed, wherefore God grew wroth, and obscured her light. Instead of shining steadily like the sun, all the length of the day, she grows old quickly, and must be born and reborn, again and again. The callous conduct of the moon offended God, not only by way of contrast with the compassion of all other creatures, but because He Himself was full of pity for Adam and his wife.[23] (Ginzberg, *Legends*, 31)

This last part about the moon is what struck me as intriguing. When we look up at the moon today it is not always a full moon and clearly it is not as bright as the sun. An interesting legend that seems true to me given the fact that everything speaks to God in their language. One thing we must understand is the fact that the sun and the moon are separate lights, the moon does not get its light from the reflecting sun. Please read the creation account found in Genesis 1.

It is my view that sin caused every disease known to man, whether physical, mental, and yes, even spiritual. Cancer, AIDS, the flu, a common cold, a child born with defects, you name it, they all came upon us as a result of sin. Earthquakes, hurricanes, tornadoes, you name it, all came to upon earth as a result of sin. However, through God's grace and mercy, and through the Blood of Jesus Christ on the cross of salvation, we can go directly to God and ask for forgiveness. And God will make a new earth and a new heaven where none of these pestilences or disasters exist. Jesus says in Revelation 21:5, "Behold, I make all things new."

The Legend of the Tunic

Here is one legend that I found quite remarkable when I read it and wondered what else could have been passed down through the generations that have since been lost to history. This one has to deal with the original clothes that God gave to Adam and Eve after they sinned:

> And the garments of skin which God made for Adam and his wife, when they went out of the garden, were given to Cush. For after the death of Adam and his wife, the garments were given to Enoch, the son of Jared, and when Enoch was taken up to God, he gave them to Methuselah, his son. And at the death of Methuselah, Noah took them and brought them to the ark, and they were with him until he went out of the ark. And in their going out, Ham stole those garments from Noah his father, and he took them and hid them from his brothers. And when Ham begat his first-born Cush, he gave him the garments in secret, and they were with Cush many days. And Cush also concealed them from his sons and brothers, and when Cush had begotten Nimrod, he gave him those garments through his love for him, and Nimrod grew up, and when he was twenty years old he put on those garments. And Nimrod became strong when he put on the garments, and God gave him might and strength, and he was a mighty hunter in the earth [Genesis 10:8–9], yea, he was a mighty

hunter in the field, and he hunted the animals and he built altars, and he offered upon them the animals before the Lord.[24] (Johnson, *Jasher*, 17)

There are those who believe that Nimrod will be reborn or raised from the dead at the end and become the Anti-Christ of the end times due to the fact that he was and is the only human to rule the entire world. You can read the **Book of Jasher** and **Legends of the Jews** to learn more about this man named Nimrod.

Adam & Eve

"Therefore the Lord God sent him out of the garden of Eden to till the ground from which he was taken. So He drove out the man…" [Genesis 3: 23–24…read ALL of Genesis Ch. 3]

"In the beginning was the Word, and the Word was with God, and the Word was God. He was in the beginning with God. All things were made through Him, and without Him nothing was made that was made. In Him was life, and the life was the light of men. And the light shines in the darkness, and the darkness did not comprehend it." [John 1:1–5]

The Altered State & The Covenant

As I mentioned in the previous chapter, everything changed when Adam and Eve sinned in the Garden of Eden, including their flesh and what they would need to do to sustain it. Let us take a look at some of these legends and see if they add up. Now, all of these legends come from **The First and Second Books of Adam and Eve**, and as I stated this is literature that someone decided to write down after hearing these, meaning passed down orally. However, if ancient texts and religious writings such as the Talmud and Koran mention some of these then there is some truth to them. These are also a part of the Pseudepigrapha.

> And indeed, when Adam looked at his flesh he saw that it was altered, and he cried bitterly, he and Eve cried over what they had done. And they walked and went gently down into the Cave of Treasures. And as they came to it, Adam cried over himself and said to Eve, 'Look at this cave that is to be our prison in this world, and a place of punishment! What is it compared with the garden? What is its narrowness compared with the space of the other? What is this rock compared of those groves? What is the gloom of this cavern, compared with the light of the garden? What is this overhanging ledge of rock that shelters us compared with the mercy of the Lord that overshadowed us? …And Adam said to Eve, 'Look at your eyes, and at mine, which before beheld angels praising in heaven without ceasing [Revelation 4:8–11]. Now we do not see as we did; our eyes have become of flesh; they cannot see like they saw before'. Adam again said to Eve, 'What is our body today, compared to what it was in former days, when we lived in the garden?'[1] (Lumpkin, *Adam & Eve*, 12)

Their bodies would surely change for the worse. "Then God the Lord said to Adam, 'When you were under subjection to Me, you had a bright nature within you and for that reason could you see distant things. But after you transgressed your bright nature was taken out of you and it was not left in you to see distant things, but only things near to you, as is the ability of the flesh, for it is brutish'."[2] Indeed, our flesh is very brutish and weak and sinful [Matthew 26:41 and Galatians 5:16–21]. We sweat, we smell unless washed, and our eyes are considered the lamp of the body [Matthew 6:22]. The flesh needs and wants things to sustain it and things that make us feel good, even things that make us sin [Romans 7:18–20]. "And Adam said, after he was raised, 'O God, while we were in the garden we did not require or care about this water, but since we came to this land we cannot do without it'. Then God said to Adam, 'While you were under My command and were a bright angel you did not experience this water. But now that you have transgressed My commandment, you can not do without water to wash your body and make it grow, for it is now like that of beasts, and is in want of water'."[3] Adam and Eve found out very quickly that what sustained them in the Garden of Eden could no longer do the same once they were driven out because of disobedience. However, because the Blood of Jesus covers sins you will never thirst again [John 4:13–14].

There is another legend that mentions a covenant between Adam and God, and it is very prophetic in what was to happen in later generations. There were many instances after they left Paradise in which Adam and Eve wanted to return to the Garden, but they are not allowed to until that covenant is fulfilled:

> Then God had pity on them, and said: 'O Adam, I have made My covenant with you, and I will not turn from it; neither will I let you return to the garden, until My covenant of the great five and a half days is fulfilled'. Then Adam said to God, 'O Lord, You created us, and made us fit to be in the garden; and before I transgressed, You made all beasts come to me, that I should name them [Genesis 2:19–20]. Your grace was then on me; and I named every one according to Your mind; and You made them all subject to me. But now, O Lord God, that I have transgressed Your commandment, all beasts will rise against me and will devour me, and Eve Your handmaid; and will cut off our life from the face of the

earth'…Then God commanded the beasts, and the birds, and all that moves on the earth, to come to Adam and to be familiar with him, and not to trouble him and Eve; nor any of the good and righteous among their offspring. Then all the beasts paid homage to Adam, according to the commandment of God except the serpent, against which God was angry. It did not come to Adam, with the beasts.[4] (Lumpkin, *Adam & Eve*, 15–16)

Here is Adam, the one that named and had dominion over the animals of earth, worried that they would try and kill him. Isn't it interesting that today there are those beasts, because of our sin, that will attack and kill a human?

Therefore God had pity on them; and when He saw them fallen before the gate of the garden, He sent His Word (Jesus) to our father Adam, and to Eve, and raised them from their fallen state. God said to Adam, 'I have ordained days and years on this earth, and you and your descendants shall live and walk in them until the days and years are fulfilled. Then I shall send the Word (Jesus) that created you and against which you have transgressed the Word (Jesus) that made you come out of the garden and that raised you when you were fallen. Yes, this is the Word (Jesus) that will again save you when the five and a half days are fulfilled' [John 1:1–3]. But when Adam heard these words from God, and of the great five and a half days he did not understand the meaning of them. For Adam was thinking there would be only five and a half days for him until the end of the world. And Adam cried and prayed to God to explain it to him. Then God in His mercy for Adam who was made after His own image [Genesis 1:26] and likeness explained to him that these were 5,000 and 500 years and how One (Jesus) would then come and save him and his descendants.[5] (Lumpkin, *Adam & Eve*, 10)

Again, Adam does not understand the fullness of what he and Eve did and how it would affect his seed until the time when One would come and save them and bring them back into Paradise. That One is Jesus, the son of God and our Savior.

There were 1,656 years that lapsed from the time Adam and Eve left the Garden of Eden until the flood of Noah (see Appendix A). What if Jesus was crucified exactly 5,500 years to the day that Adam and Eve were kicked out of the Garden of Eden? Would you believe on Him then?

The Fall of Satan

When Adam and Eve were kicked out of the Garden of Eden they came to a place where satan was already dwelling. It was satan inside the serpent that deceived them in the garden. Satan tried to do the same thing in Job 1:6–12:

> Now there was a day when the sons of God came to present themselves before the Lord, and satan also came among them. And the Lord said to satan, 'From where do you come?' So satan answered the Lord and said, 'From going to and fro on the earth, and from walking back and forth on it.' Then the Lord said to satan, 'Have you considered My servant Job, that there is none like him on the earth, a blameless and upright man, one who fears God and shuns evil?' So satan answered the Lord and said, 'Does Job fear God for nothing? Have you not made a hedge around him, around his household, and around all that he has on every side? You have blessed the work of his hands, and his possessions have increased in the land. But now, stretch out Your hand and touch all that he has, and he will surely curse You to Your face!' And the Lord said to satan, 'Behold, all that he has is in your power; only do not lay a hand on his person.' So satan went out from the presence of the Lord. (NKJV)

There are legends of a 'feathered serpent' or 'dragon' going to different civilizations on earth in ancient times, bringing with him knowledge. He is known to the Aztecs as Quetzalcoatl, to the Mayans as Kukulkan, to the Incas as Viracocha, to the Norse he is known as Nidhogg Nagar, he is known as Naga in Hindu and Buddhist lore, and in ancient China as Long or Lung. In Hinduism, their gods Vishnu and Shiva are said to have ridden on a serpent. There is the 'Temple of the Feathered Serpent' in the ancient city of Chichen Itza. To me, this 'feathered serpent' is the same satan who tempted Adam and Eve and the same one who went 'to and fro' [Genesis 8:6–7 and Job 1:7]. Satan, or the adversary, seeks to deceive the world of its true creation, and of the One God.

But how did satan get here? The answer is that he was thrown down to earth because of his disobedience and wanting to be equal with his Creator. Luke 10:18–20 states, "And He said to them, 'I saw satan fall like lightning from heaven. Behold, I give you the authority to trample on serpents and scorpions, and over all the power of the enemy, and nothing shall by any means hurt you. Nevertheless do not rejoice in this, that the spirits are subject to you, but rather rejoice because your names are written in heaven'." And again, Isaiah 14:12–15 states, "How you are fallen from heaven, o Lucifer, son of the morning! How you are cut down to the ground, you who weakened the nations! For you have said in your heart, 'I will ascend into heaven, I will exalt my throne above the stars of God; I will also sit on the mount of the congregation on the farthest sides of the north; I will ascend above the heights of the clouds, I will be like the Most High.' Yet you shall be brought down to Sheol, to the lowest depths of the pit."

So, we just read a couple of reports from the Bible of how satan fell to earth but let us take a look at a few others:

> Then the angels said to Adam, 'You obeyed satan and ignored the Word of God (Jesus) who created you. You believed that satan would fulfill all he had promised you. But now, Adam, we will make known to you what came over us through him, before his fall from heaven. He gathered together his hosts and deceived them, promising to give them a great kingdom, a divine nature, and other promises he made them. His hosts believed that his word was true, so they followed him, and renounced the glory

of God. He then ordered us, and some obeyed and under his command, and accepted his empty promises. But we would not obey and we did not take his orders. Then, after he had fought with God and had dealt disrespectfully with Him, he gathered together his hosts and made war with us. And if it had not been for God's strength that was with us we could not have prevailed against him to hurl him from heaven [Revelation 12:7–12]. But when he fell from among us there was great joy in heaven because of his descent from us. If he had remained in heaven, nothing, not even one angel would have remained in it. But God in His mercy drove him from among us to this dark earth because he had become darkness itself and a performer of unrighteousness. And Adam, he has continued to make war against you until he tricked you and made you come out of the garden to this strange land, where all these trials have come to you. And death, which God brought to him, he has also brought to you because you obeyed him and sinned against God'…Then the Word of God (Jesus) came to Adam, and said to him…'If you had submitted and been obedient to Me and had kept My Word, you would be with My angels in My garden. But when you sinned and obeyed satan, you became his guests among his angels [John 12:31 and 1 John 5:19], that are full of wickedness, and you came to this earth that produces thorns and thistles for you [Genesis 3:17–19]. O Adam, ask the one who deceived you to give you the divine nature he promised you, or to make you a garden as I had made for you, or to fill you with that same bright nature with which I had filled you. Ask him to make you a body like the one I made you, or to give you a day of rest as I gave you, or to create within you a wise soul, as I created for you; or to take you from here to some other earth than this one which I gave you. But, Adam, he will not fulfill even one of the things he told you. Acknowledge My favor towards you, and My mercy on you, My creature.

Acknowledge that I have not shown vengeance on you for your transgression against Me, but in My pity for you I have promised you that at the end of the great five and a half days I will come and save you'…But Adam's heart was comforted by God's words to him, and he worshipped before Him. And God commended His angels to escort Adam and Eve to the cave with joy instead of the fear that had come over them…there the angels began to comfort and to strengthen them, and then departed from them towards heaven to their Creator, who had sent them. But after the angels had departed from Adam and Eve, satan came with shamefacedness and stood at the entrance of the cave in which were Adam and Eve. He then called to Adam, and said, 'O Adam, come, let me speak to you.' Then Adam came out of the cave, thinking he was one of God's angels that had come to give him some good counsel. But when Adam came out and saw his hideous figure he was afraid of him, and said to him, 'Who are you?' Then satan answered and said to him, 'It is I, who hid myself within the serpent, and who spoke to Eve, and who enticed her until she obeyed my command. I am he who, using my deceitful speech, sent her to deceive you until you both ate of the fruit of the tree and rejected the command of God.' But when Adam heard these words from him, he said to him, 'Can you make me a garden as God made for me? Or can you clothe me in the same bright nature in which God had clothed me? Where is the divine nature you promised to give me? Where is that clever speech of yours that you had with us at first, when we were in the garden?' Then satan said to Adam, 'Do you think that when I have promised someone something that I would actually deliver it to him or fulfill my word? Of course not. I myself have no hope of obtaining what I promised. Therefore I fell, and I made you fall for the same reason that I myself fell. Whoever accepts my counsel, falls. But now, O Adam, because you fell you are under my rule [John 12:31]…because you have obeyed me and have sinned against your God. There will be no deliverance from my hands until the day promised you by your God.' Again he said, ' Because we do not know the day agreed on with you by your God, nor the hour in which you shall be delivered [Acts 1:7], we will multiply wars and murders on you and your descendants after you [Matthew 24:36 and 1 Peter 5:8]. This is our will and our good pleasure that we may not leave on of the sons of men to inherit our place in heaven. Our home, Adam, is in the burning fire and we will not stop our evil doing even a single day nor even a single hour…' [Revelation 12:1–17]. [6] (Lumpkin, *Adam & Eve*, 74–78)

Therefore, He sent His Word (Jesus) to them that they should stand and be raised immediately. And the Lord said to Adam and Eve, 'You transgressed of your own free will, until you came out of the garden in which I had placed you. Of your own free will have you transgressed through your desire for divinity, greatness, and an exalted state, such as I have; therefore I deprived you of the bright nature which you had then, and I made you come out of the garden [Genesis 3:23] to this land, rough and full of trouble. If only you had not transgressed My commandment and had kept My law, and had not eaten of the fruit of the tree which I told you not to come near! And there were fruit trees in the garden better than that one. But the wicked satan did not keep his faith and had no good intent towards Me, and although I had created him he considered Me to be useless, and he sought the Godhead for himself. For this I hurled him down from heaven [Isaiah 14:12–15] so that he could not remain in his first estate. It was he who made the tree appear pleasant to your eyes [Genesis 3:1–6] until you ate of it by believing his words. Thus have you transgressed My commandment, and therefore I have brought on you all these sorrows. For I am God the Creator, who, when I created My creatures, did not intend to destroy them'.[7] (Lumpkin, *Adam & Eve*, 14–15)

Now, God will explain to Adam what separates light from darkness and the reason behind free will. In reality, Adam was afraid of the night because he knew not the night while in the garden and in the presence of his Creator [Revelation 22:5].

Then when God, who is merciful and full of pity, heard Adam's voice, He said to him: 'O Adam, so long as the good angel was obedient to Me, a bright light rested on him and on his hosts. But when he transgressed My commandment, I dispossessed him of that bright nature, and he became dark. And when he was in the heavens, in the realms of light, he knew nothing of darkness. But he transgressed, and I made him fall from the heaven onto the earth [Revelation 12:8–9]; and it was this darkness that came over him. And, O Adam, while in My garden and obedient to Me that bright light rest also on you. But when I heard of your transgression, I took from you that bright light. Yet, of My mercy, I did not turn you into darkness but I made your body a body of flesh over which I spread this skin in order that it may bear cold and heat. If I had let My wrath fall heavily on you I should have destroyed you and had I turned you into darkness it would have been as if I had killed you…Thus, O Adam, has this night deceived you. It is not to last forever but is only of twelve hours when it is over daylight will return… Strengthen your heart and be not afraid. This darkness is not a punishment. Adam, I have made the day and have placed the sun in it to give light [Genesis 1:16] in order that you and your children should do your work. For I knew you would sin and transgress and come out into this land…For I made you of the light and I willed to bring out children of light from you that were like you.

But you did not keep My commandment one day until I had finished the creation and blessed everything in it. Then, concerning the tree, I commanded you not to eat of it [Genesis 2:16]. Yet I knew that satan, who deceived himself, would also deceive you. So I made known to you by means of the tree, not to come near him. And I told you not to eat of the fruit thereof, nor to taste it, nor yet to sit under it, nor yet to yield to it. Had I not spoken to you, O Adam, concerning the tree and had I left you without a commandment and you had sinned it would have been an offence on My part, for not having given you any order you would turn around and blame Me for it. But I commanded you, and warned you, and you fell. So that My creatures cannot blame Me; but the blame rests on them alone. And, O Adam, I have made the day so that you and your descendants can work and toil in it. And I have made the night for them to rest in it from their work…'[8] (Lumpkin, *Adam & Eve*, 21–23)

Ever since satan fell to earth his number one goal has been to deceive mankind and bring them under his dominion and ultimately, into hell.

Jesus Himself was even tempted by satan in the desert after His baptism. We read in Luke 4:1–13:

"Then Jesus, being filled with the Holy Spirit, returned from the Jordan and was led by the Spirit into the wilderness, being tempted for forty days by the devil. And in those days He ate nothing, and afterward, when they had ended, He was hungry. And the devil said to Him, 'If You are the Son of God, command this stone to become bread.' But Jesus answered him, saying, 'It is written, 'Man shall not live by bread alone, but by every word of God'.' Then the devil, taking Him up on a high mountain, showed Him all the kingdoms of the world in a moment of time. And the devil said to Him, 'All this authority I will give to You, and their glory; for this has been delivered to me, and I give it to whomever I wish. Therefore, if You will worship before me, all will be Yours'. And Jesus answered and said to him, 'Get behind Me, satan! For it is written, 'You shall worship the Lord your God, and Him only you shall serve'.' Then he brought Him to Jerusalem, set Him on the pinnacle of the temple, and said to Him, 'If You are the Son of God, throw Yourself down from here. For it is written, 'He shall give His angels charge over you, to keep you', and, 'In their hands they shall bear you up, lest you dash your foot against a stone'.' And Jesus answered and said to him, 'It has been said, 'You shall not tempt the Lord your God'.' Now when the devil had ended every temptation, he departed from Him until an opportune time." (NKJV)

So, if the adversary tried to deceive and tempt Jesus, although the Son of God knew who it was and satan knew who he was trying to deceive, it would be reasonable to think he would try to deceive us as well. He has succeeded in deceiving many throughout the generations of man as evidenced when Jesus says in Matthew 7:13–14, "Enter by the narrow gate; for wide is the gate and broad is the way that leads to destruction, and there are many who go in by it. Because narrow is the gate and difficult is the way which leads to life, and there are few who find it." Do not be deceived, Jesus is the answer.

God v. Satan

God is light [Psalm 119:105 and 1 John 1:5] and satan is darkness. The adversary, or satan, is powerless in the presence of God and His Light. John 1:5 says, "And the light shines in the darkness, and the darkness did not comprehend it." Jesus Himself states in John 8:12, "Then Jesus spoke to them again, saying, 'I am the light of the world. He who follows Me shall not walk in darkness, but have the light of life'."

Here is a story of the serpent trying to kill Adam and Eve:

Then, Adam and Eve came out at the mouth of the cave and went toward the garden. But as they went near the western gate, from which satan came when he deceived Adam and Eve, they found the serpent that became satan [Revelation 12:9] coming at the gate, and it was sorrowfully licking the dust, and wiggling on its breast on the ground because of the curse that fell on it from God [Genesis 3:14–15]. Before the curse the serpent was the most exalted of all beasts, now it was changed and become slippery and the meanest of them all, and it crept on its breast and went on its belly. Before, it was the fairest of all beasts. It had been changed and became the most ugly of them all. Instead of feeding on the best food, now it turned to eat the dust. Instead of living as before, in the best places, now it lived in the dust. It had been the most beautiful of all beasts, and all stood speechless at its beauty, it was now abhorred of them. And, again, whereas it lived in a beautiful home, to which all other animals came from everywhere; and where it drank, they drank also of the same; now, after it had become venomous, by reason of God's curse, all beasts fled from its home and would not drink of the water it drank, but fled from it. When the accursed serpent saw Adam and Eve it swelled its head, stood on its tail, and with eyes blood-red, it acted like it would kill them. It made straight for Eve and ran after her while Adam stood by and yelled because he had no stick in his hand with which to hit the serpent, and did not know how to put it to death. But with a heart burning for Eve, Adam approached the serpent and held it by the tail. When it turned towards him and said to him: 'O Adam, because of you and Eve I am slippery, and go on my belly.' Then with its great strength it threw down Adam and Eve and squeezed them, and tried to kill them. But God sent an angel who threw the serpent away from them, and raised them up. Then the Word of God (Jesus) came to the serpent, and said to it, 'The first time I made you slick, and made you to go on your belly but I did not deprive you of speech. This time, however, you will be mute, and you and your race will speak no more because, the first time My creatures were ruined because of you, and this time you tried to kill them.' Then the serpent was struck mute, and it was no longer able to speak."[9] (Lumpkin, *Adam & Eve*, 25–27)

As we can see, satan has to obey the voice and commands of his Creator.

Once they left the garden Adam and Eve were under the rule of satan and many times he tried to deceive them and hurt them. Here are three separate accounts:

Then Adam stood and asked God to show him something with which to cover their bodies. Then came the Word of God (Jesus) and said to him, 'O Adam, take Eve and come to the seashore, where you fasted before. There you will find skins of sheep that were left after lions ate the carcasses. Take them and make garments for yourselves and clothe yourselves with them' [Genesis 3:21]. When Adam heard these words from God, he took Eve and went from the northern side of the garden to the south of it, by the river of water where they once fasted. But as they were on their way, and before they arrived, satan, the wicked one, had heard the Word of God (Jesus) communing with Adam respecting his covering. It distressed him, and he hurried to the place where the sheepskins were, with the intension of taking them and throwing them into the sea or of burning them so that Adam and Eve would not find them. But as he was about to take them, the Word of God (Jesus) came from heaven and bound him by the side of those skins until Adam and Eve came near him. But as they got closer to him they were afraid of him and his hideous appearance. Then the Word of God (Jesus) came to Adam and Eve, and said to them, 'This is he who was hidden in the serpent, who deceived you, and stripped from you your garment of light and glory. This is he who promised you majesty and divinity. Where is the beauty that was on him? Where is his divinity? Where is his light? Where is the glory that rested on him? Now his form is hideous. He has become abominable among angels, and he has come to be called satan. Adam, he wished to steal from you this earthly garment of sheepskins so that he could destroy it and not let you be covered with it. What is his beauty that you should have followed him? And what have you gained by obeying him? See his evil works and then look at Me, your Creator. Look at the good deeds I do for you. I bound him until you came and saw and his weakness and that no power is left with him.'[10] (Lumpkin, *Adam & Eve*, 68–69)

It is very prophetic that God would have lions eat the sheep and then clothe Adam and Eve with their skins. John 1:29–30 states, "The next day John saw Jesus coming toward him, and said, 'Behold! The Lamb of God who takes away the sin of the world! This is He of whom I said, 'After me comes a Man who is preferred before me, for He was before me'.'" And 1 Peter 5:8 reads, "Be sober, be vigilant; because your adversary the devil walks about like a roaring lion, seeking whom he may devour." You see, there has to be a sacrifice for sin, and Christ Jesus was that sacrifice. Jesus is the Lamb of God, that perfect sacrifice.

satan, the hater of all that is good, saw how they continued in prayer, and how God communed with them, and comforted them, and how he had accepted their offering. The satan made a phantasm. He began by transforming his hosts. In his hands was a shining, glimmering fire, and they were in a huge light. Then, he placed his throne near the mouth of the cave, because he could not enter it due to their prayers. And he shown light into the cave until the cave glistened over Adam and Eve while his hosts began to sing praises. satan did this so that when Adam saw the light he would think to himself that it was a heavenly light and that satan's hosts were angels and that God had sent them to watch at the cave, and give him light in the darkness. satan planned that when Adam came out of the cave and saw them and Adam and Eve bowed to satan, then he would overcome Adam and humble him before God a second time. When, therefore, Adam and Eve saw the light, thinking it was real, they strengthened their hearts. Then, as they were trembling, Adam said to Eve, 'Look at that great light, and at those many songs of praise, and at that host standing outside who won't come into our cave. Why don't they tell us what they want or where they are from or what the meaning of this light is or what those praises are or why they have been sent to this place, and why they won't come in? If they were from God, they would come into the cave with us and would tell us why they were sent.' Then Adam stood up and prayed to God with a burning heart and said: 'O Lord, is there in the world another god besides You who created angels and filled them with light, and sent them to keep us, who would come with them? But, look, we see these hosts that stand at the mouth of the cave. They are in a great light and they sing loud praises. If they are of some other god than You, tell me, and if they are sent by You, inform me of the reason for which You have sent them.' No sooner had Adam said this, than an angel from God appeared to him in the cave, who said to him, 'O Adam, fear not. This is satan and his hosts. He wishes to deceive you as he deceived you at first. For the first time, he was hidden in the serpent, but this time he is come to you in the likeness of an angel of light [2 Corinthians 11:14] in order that, when you worshipped him, he might enslave you in the very presence of God.' Then the angel went from Adam and seized satan at the opening of the cave, and stripped him of the false image he had assumed and brought him in his own hideous form to Adam and Eve who were afraid of him when they saw him. And the angel said to Adam, 'This hideous form has been his ever since God made him fall from heaven. He could not have come near you in it. Therefore he transforms himself into an angel of light.'[11] (Lumpkin, *Adam & Eve*, 37–38)

The name Lucifer literally means 'light-bearer'. Isaiah 14:12–15 says, "How you are fallen from heaven, O Lucifer, son of the morning! How you are cut down to the ground, you who weakened the nations! For you have said in your heart: 'I will ascend into heaven, I will exalt my throne above the stars of God; I will also sit on the mount of the congregation on the farthest sides of the north; I will ascend above the heights of the clouds, I will be like the Most High.' Yet you shall be brought down to Sheol, to the lowest depths of the Pit."

The God sent His Word (Jesus) to Adam, saying, 'Adam, that apparition is the one that promised you the Godhead, and majesty. He does not intend good for you, but shows himself to you at one time in the form of a woman and in another moment in the likeness of an angel, and on another occasion in the apparition of a serpent, and at another time in the semblance of a god. But he does all of this only to destroy your soul [1 Peter 5:8]. Adam, now that you understand this in your heart you will see that I have delivered you many a time from his hands in order to show you that I am a merciful God. I wish you good and I do not wish you ruin' [Isaiah 41:10, Romans 15:13, and John 16:33]. Then God ordered satan to show himself to Adam in his own hideous form, plainly. But when Adam saw him he feared and trembled at the sight of him. And God said to Adam, 'Look at this devil, and at his hideous sight, and know that he it is who made you fall from brightness into darkness, from peace and rest to toil and misery. And look at him, Adam. He is the one that said that he is God! Can God be black? Would God take the form of a woman? Is there any one stronger than God?

And can He be overpowered? See Adam. Look at him bound in your presence, in the air, unable to flee away! So, I say to you, do not be afraid of him. From now on, take care, and beware of him. He will try to do things to you.' Then God drove satan away from Adam. And God strengthened Adam's heart and comforted him, saying, 'Go down to the Cave of Treasures, and do not separate yourself from Eve. I will quiet all of your animal lust.' From that hour it left Adam and Eve, and they enjoyed rest by the commandment of God. But God did not do the same to any of Adam's seed. God did this only to Adam and Eve.[12] (Lumpkin, *Adam & Eve*, 130–131)

God would leave everything to Adam and Eve. They would be the ones to tell their offspring of the true Creator and of the one who seeks to deceive them.

Satan has been trying to deceive humans about their Creator since Adam and Eve were kicked out of the garden [1 John 3:8 and John 8:44]. As you just read, he can transform into anything because this is his domain [Ephesians 2:2]. He wants to destroy your immortal soul, and your soul is immortal, but you have a choice. Do you want to live eternally in hell where there is 'gnashing of teeth' [Matthew 13:41–42 and Luke 13:28], where it is always hot and cold and dark, and where God and His light are nowhere to be found? Or do you want to be in the presence of the One who created you, the One who knew you before creation [Daniel 12:1 and Revelation 20:15], and the One who knitted you together in your mother's womb [Psalm 139:13–14], in heaven. I do not know about you, but I choose eternal life with Jesus in heaven and you can to if you just admit that you are a sinful creature who needs forgiveness and ask that Jesus come into your heart. He will transform you and make you a new creature. 2 Corinthians 5:17 says, "Therefore, if anyone is in Christ, he is a new creation; old things have passed away; behold, all things have become new."

Enoch, the Fallen Angels and Giants

"Enoch lived sixty-five years, and begot Methuselah. After he begot Methuselah, Enoch walked with God three hundred years, and had sons and daughters. So all the days of Enoch were three hundred and sixty-five years. And Enoch walked with God; and he was not, for God took him." [Genesis 5: 21–24]

"Now Enoch, the seventh from Adam, prophesied about these men also, saying, 'Behold, the Lord comes with ten thousands of His saints, to execute judgment on all, to convict all who are ungodly among them of all their ungodly deeds which they have committed in an ungodly way, and of all the harsh things which ungodly sinners have spoken against Him'." [Jude v.14–15]

"By faith Enoch was taken away so that he did not see death, 'and was not found, because God had taken him', for before he was taken he had this testimony, that he pleased God." [Hebrews 11: 5]

"Now it came to pass, when men began to multiply on the face of the earth, and daughters were born to them, that the sons of God saw the daughters of men, that they were beautiful; and they took wives for themselves of all whom they chose...there were giants on the earth in those days, and also afterward, when the sons of God came in to the daughters of men and they bore children to them. Those were the mighty men who were of old, men of renown." [Genesis 6: 1–2, 4]

"And the angels who did not keep their proper domain, but left their own abode, He has reserved in everlasting chains under darkness for the judgment of the great day..." [Jude v.6]

"For if God did not spare the angels who sinned, but cast them down to hell and delivered them into chains of darkness, to be reserved for judgment" [2 Peter 2:4]

The Man

"…For Enoch's office was ordained for a testimony to the generations of the world, so that he should recount all the deeds of generation unto generation, till the day of judgment."[1]

It is my belief that Enoch is one of the two witnesses from the book of Revelation and the other is the prophet Elijah. Now, most theologians will say that it is Moses and Elijah, but Moses died in the desert before the Israelites entered into the Promised Land [Deuteronomy 34:1–8]. Neither Enoch [Genesis 5:24] nor Elijah [2 Kings 2:11] died an earthly death and all men must do so because of sin. Hebrews 9:27–28 states, "And as it is appointed for men to die once, but after this the judgment, so Christ was offered once to bear the sins of many. To those who eagerly wait for Him He will appear a second time, apart from sin, for salvation." 1 Corinthians 15:50–52 says, "Now this I say, brethren, that flesh and blood cannot inherit the kingdom of God; nor does corruption inherit incorruption. Behold, I tell you a mystery: We shall not all sleep, but we shall all be changed – in a moment, in the twinkling of an eye, at the last trumpet. For the trumpet will sound, and the dead will be raised incorruptible, and we shall be changed." The only humans who will not have to die an earthly death are those who believe in Jesus when he comes back to take His Church to where He is. 1 Thessalonians 4:16–17 says, "For the Lord Himself will descend from heaven with a shout, with the voice of an archangel, and with the trumpet of God. And the dead in Christ will rise first. Then we who are alive and remain shall be caught up together with them in the clouds to meet the Lord in the air. And thus we shall always be with the Lord." For this reason, I believe the so-called rapture takes place after the two witnesses are killed. Revelation 11:3–6 states, "And I will give power to My two witnesses, and they will prophesy one thousand two hundred and sixty days, clothed in sackcloth'. These are the two olive trees and the two lampstands standing before the God of the earth. And if anyone wants to harm them, fire proceeds from their mouth and devours their enemies. And if anyone wants to harm them, he must be killed in this manner. These have power to shut heaven, so that no rain falls in the days of their prophecy; and they have power over waters to turn them to blood, and to strike the earth with all plagues, as often as they desire."

Enoch was the seventh from Adam [Jude 1:14] through the lineage of Seth [Genesis 5:1–24], who replaced Abel [Genesis 4:25]. Here are several accounts that tell us what Enoch wrote down: "And now, my son Methuselah, all these things I am recounting to you and writing down for you! And I have revealed to you everything, and given you books concerning all these; so, my son Methuselah, preserve the books from your father's hand, and see that you deliver them to the generations of the world. I have given wisdom to you and to your children, and those children to come, that they may give it to their children for generations."[2]

Enoch would keep the command from his father, Jared, and would be a minister to the people of the world, "Enoch kept the commandment of Jared his father, and continued to minister in the cave. Many wonders happened to this man, Enoch, and he also wrote a celebrated book; but those wonders may not be told in this place."[3]

And he was the first among men that are born on earth who learnt writing and knowledge and wisdom and who wrote down the signs of heaven according to the order of their months in a book, that men might know the seasons of the years according to the order of their separate months. And he was the first to write a testimony, and he testified to the sons of men among the generations of the earth, and recounted the weeks of the jubilees, and made known to them the days of the years, and set in order the months and recounted the Sabbaths of the years as we made them known to him. And what was and what will be he saw in a vision of his sleep, as it will happen to the children of men throughout their generations until the day of judgment; he saw and understood everything, and wrote his testimony, and placed the testimony on earth for all the children of men and for their generations...And he was moreover with the angels of God these six jubilees of years [Genesis 5:22], and they showed him everything which is on earth and in the heavens, the rule of the sun, and he wrote down everything. And he testified to the Watchers, who had sinned with the daughters of men

[Genesis 6:2]; for these had begun to unite themselves, so as to be defiled, with the daughters of men, and Enoch testified against them all. And he was taken from amongst the children of men [Genesis 5:24], and we conducted him into the Garden of Eden in majesty and honour, and behold there he writeth down the condemnation and judgment of the world, and all the wickedness of the children of men…for there he was as a sign and that he should testify against all the children of men, that he should recount all the deeds of the generations until the day of condemnation [Jude 1:14–15]. [4] (Johnson, *Jubilees*, 24–25)

Once…while he sojourned among men, he had been permitted to see all there is on earth and in the heavens. On a time when he was sleeping, a great grief came upon his heart, and he wept in his dream, not knowing what the grief meant, nor what would happen to him. And there appeared to him two men, very tall. Their faces shone like the sun, and their eyes were like burning lamps, and fire came forth from their lips; their wings were brighter than gold, their hands whiter than snow. They stood at the head of Enoch's bed, and called him by his name. He awoke from his sleep, and hastened and made obeisance to them, and was terrified. And these men said to him: 'Be of good cheer, Enoch, be not afraid; the everlasting God hath sent us to thee, and lo! Today thou shalt ascend with us into heaven. And tell thy sons and thy servants, and let none seek thee, till the Lord bring thee back to them'…these two men summoned him, and took him on their wings, and placed him on the clouds, which moved higher and higher, till they set him down in the first heaven. Here they showed him the two hundred angels who rule the stars, and their heavenly service. Here he saw also the treasuries of snow and ice, of clouds and dew [Genesis 7:11]. From here they took him to the second heaven, where he saw the fallen angels imprisoned... They took him from thence to the third heaven, where they showed him Paradise, with all the trees of beautiful colors, and their fruits, ripe and luscious, and all kinds of food which they produced, springing up with delightful fragrance...He also saw the three hundred angels who keep the Garden, and with never-ceasing voices and blessed singing they serve the Lord every day. The angels leading Enoch explained to him that this place is prepared for the righteous, while the terrible place prepared for the sinners is in the northern regions of the third heaven. He saw there all sorts of tortures, and impenetrable gloom, and there is no light there [Job 18:5 and Matthew 8:12], but a gloomy fire is always burning. And all that place has fire on all sides [Psalm 21:8–9], and on all sides cold and ice, thus it burns and freezes. And the angels, terrible and without pity, carry savage weapons, and their torture is unmerciful [Luke 16:19–31]. The angels took him thence to the fourth heaven, and showed him all the comings in and goings forth, and all the rays of the light of the sun and the moon...They showed him also the six gates in the east of the fourth heaven, by which the sun goes forth, and the six gates in the west where he sets, and also the gates by which the moon goes out, and those by which she enters. In the middles of the fourth heaven he saw an armed host, serving the Lord with cymbals and organs and unceasing voices...In the seventh heaven he saw the seven bands of archangels who arrange and study the revolutions of the stars and the changes of the moon and the revolution of the sun, and superintended the good or evil conditions of the world. And they arrange teachings and instructions and sweet speaking and singing and all kinds of glorious praise...When Enoch reached the seventh heaven, and saw all the fiery hosts of great archangels and incorporeal powers and lordships and principalities and powers, he was afraid and trembled with a great terror. Those leading him took hold of him, and brought him into the midst of them, and said to him, 'Be of good cheer, Enoch, be not afraid', and they showed him the Lord from afar, sitting on His lofty throne [Revelation 4:2], while all the heavenly hosts, divided in ten classes, having approached, stood on the ten steps according to their rank.[5] (Ginzberg, *Legends*, 47–48)

If you want to know all of what Enoch saw and wrote down please read the Book of Enoch, as the first Church did. They thought of it as 'inspired'.

Enoch knew everything, and I mean everything, hence the reason he was taken. He was taught by the angels and God Himself. Enoch had the spirit of God resting on him:

And the soul of Enoch was wrapped up in the instruction of the Lord, in knowledge and in understanding; and he wisely retired from the sons of men, and secreted himself from them for many days. And it was at the expiration of many years, whilst he was serving the Lord, and praying before him in his house, that an angel of the Lord called to him from heaven, and he said, 'Here am I' [1 Samuel 3]. And he said, 'Rise, go forth from thy house and from the place where thou dost hide thyself, and appear to the sons of men, in order that thou mayest teach them the way in which they should go and the work which they must accomplish to enter in the ways of God'... And the spirit of God was upon Enoch, and he taught all his men the wisdom of God and His ways, and the sons of men served the Lord all the days of Enoch, and they came to hear his wisdom. And all the kings of the sons of men, both first and last, together with their princes and judges, came to Enoch when they heard of his wisdom, and they bowed down to him, and they also required of Enoch to reign over them, to which he consented...And Enoch taught them wisdom, knowledge, and the ways of the Lord; and he made peace amongst them, and peace was throughout the earth during the life of Enoch. And Enoch reigned over the sons of men two hundred and forty-three years, and he did justice and righteousness with all his people, and he led them in the ways of the Lord.[6] (Johnson, *Jasher*, 10)

We see that the men of the earth wanted Enoch to be their king and ruler because of his wisdom, understanding, and connection to God. Enoch reminds me of king Solomon in this aspect because the kings and princes came to hear the wisdom of Solomon as well [2 Chronicles 9:1–28].

The Teachings

Enoch was the first prophet [Jude 1:14] and nearly all of his prophecies dealt with the generations of a future time to come. Let us look at some of these accounts: "And this is the beginning of the words of wisdom which I lifted up my voice to speak and say to those which dwell on earth: 'Hear, you men of old time, and see, you that come after, the words of the Holy One which I will speak before the Lord of spirits [Isaiah 11:2, Revelation 3:1 and 4:5]. The words are for the men of old time, and to those that come after. We will not withhold the beginning of wisdom from this present day. Such wisdom has never been given by the Lord of spirits as I have received according to my insight, according to the good pleasure [1 John 5:14] of the Lord of spirits by whom the lot of eternal life has been given to me'."[7]

> After Enoch had lived a long time secluded from men, he once heard the voice of an angel calling to him: 'Enoch, Enoch, make thyself ready and leave the house and the secret place wherein thou hast kept thyself hidden, and assume dominion over men, to teach them they ways in which they shall walk, and the deeds which they shall do, in order that they may walk in the ways of God' [Exodus 18:20, Psalm 1:1–3, and 1 John 2:3–6]. Enoch left his retreat and betook himself to the haunts of men. He gathered them about him, and instructed them in the conduct pleasing to God...Thereupon a vast concourse of

people thronged about him, to hear the wisdom he would teach and learn from his mouth what is good and right. Even kings and princes, no less than one hundred and thirty in number, assembled about him, and submitted themselves to his dominion, to be taught and guided by him, as he taught and guided all the others. Peace reigned thus over the whole world all the two hundred and forty-three years during which the influence of Enoch prevailed.[8] (Ginzberg, *Legends*, 46)

Enoch said also to them, 'Watch over your souls, and hold tight to your fear of God and your service to Him, and worship Him in righteous faith, and serve Him in righteousness, innocence and judgment. Worship Him in repentance and in purity' [Deuteronomy 10:12–14]. When Enoch had ended his commandments to them, God transported him from that mountain to the land of life, to the mansions of the righteous and of the chosen ones [John 14:1–2], which is the abode of Paradise of joy, in light that reaches up to heaven. It is the light that is beyond the light of this world. It is the light of God [Revelation 21:22–24] that fills the whole world, and no place can contain. Enoch was in the light of God [1 Thessalonians 5:4–5] and because of this he found himself out of the grasp of death [Hebrews 11:5], until God would have him die.[9] (Lumpkin, *Adam & Eve*, 171)

He taught the generations of men to fear God in all aspects of life. He taught them to walk in His ways just as he was doing. He also taught them about everlasting life and about the Holy One who would come and save them if they continued to follow the instructions of the Lord.

Enoch, as well as Elijah, will die an earthly death at the end, but they will be resurrected after three and a half days. Revelation 11:7–12 says:

"When they finish their testimony, the beast that ascends out of the bottomless pit will make war against them, overcome them, and kill them. And their dead bodies will lie in the street of the great city which spiritually is called Sodom and Egypt, where also our Lord was crucified. Then those from the peoples, tribes, tongues, and nations will see their dead bodies three and a half days, and not allow their dead bodies to be put into graves. And those who dwell on the earth will rejoice over them, make merry, and send gifts to one another, because these two prophets tormented those who dwell on the earth. Now after three and a half days the breath of life from God entered them, and they stood on their feet, and great fear fell on those who saw them. And they heard a loud voice from heaven saying to them, 'Come up here'. And they ascended to heaven in a cloud, and their enemies saw them." (NKJV)

The Ascension

Genesis 5:24 states, "And Enoch walked with God; and he was not, for God took him." We know that Elijah was taken up [2 Kings 2:11], but did Enoch go up in the same way? As a matter of fact he did:

> And it was in the fifty-sixth year of the life of Lamech when Adam died; nine hundred and thirty years old was he at his death, and his two sons, with Enoch and Methuselah his son, buried him with great pomp, as at the burial of kings, in the cave which God had told him...And it was in the year of Adam's death which was the two hundred and forty-third year of the reign of Enoch, in that time Enoch resolved to separate himself from the sons of men and to secret himself as at first in order to serve the Lord...And he did in this manner for many years, and he afterward concealed himself for six days, and appeared to his people one day in seven; and after that once in a month, and then once in a year, until all the kings, princes and sons of men sought for him, and desired again to see the face of Enoch, and to hear his word; but they could not, as all

the sons of men were greatly afraid of Enoch, and they feared to approach him on account of the Godlike awe that was seated upon his countenance; therefore no man could look at him, fearing he might be punished and die…And in some time after, when the kings and princes and the sons of men were speaking to Enoch, and Enoch was teaching them the ways of God, behold an angel of the Lord then called unto Enoch from heaven, and wished to bring him up to heaven to make him reign there over the sons of God, as he had reigned over the sons of men upon earth. When at that time Enoch heard this he went and assembled all the inhabitants of the earth, and taught them wisdom and knowledge and gave them divine instructions, and he said to them, 'I have been required to ascend into heaven, I therefore do not know the day of my going'.[10] (Johnson, *Jasher*, 11)

Enoch knew he was to ascend to heaven, but he did not know when. Jesus Himself does not even know when He is coming back. Mark 13:32–33 says, "But of that day and hour no one knows, not even the angels in heaven, nor the Son, but only the Father. Take heed, watch and pray; for you do not know when the time is." Also, Matthew 24:36 states, "But of that day and hour no one knows, not even the angels of heaven, but My Father only." Enoch knew what to look for, or the signs of his going, leading up to his ascension into heaven. We also, were given signs to look for before the coming of the Son of Man [Matthew 24].

Here are a couple of the actual accounts of what happened when Enoch left this earth:

And he taught them wisdom and knowledge, and gave them instruction, and he reproved them, and he placed before them statutes and judgments to do upon earth, and he made peace amongst them, and he taught them everlasting life, and dwelt with them some time teaching them all these things. And at that time the sons of men were with Enoch, and Enoch was speaking to them, and they lifted up their eyes and the likeness of a great horse descended from heaven, and the horse paced in the air; And they told Enoch what they had seen, and Enoch said to them, 'On my account does this horse descend upon earth; the time is come when I must go from you and I shall no more be seen by you'. And the horse descended at that time and stood before Enoch, and all the sons of men that were with Enoch saw him…And it was after this that he rose up and rode upon the horse; and he went forth and all the sons of men went after him, about eight hundred thousand men; and they went with him one day's journey. And the second day he said to them, 'Return home to your tents, why will you go? Perhaps you may die'; and some of them went from him, and those that remained went with him six day's journey; and Enoch said to them every day, 'Return to your tents, lest you may die'; but they were not willing to return, and they went with him. And on the sixth day some of the men remained and clung to him, and they said to him, 'We will go with thee to the place where thou goest; as the Lord liveth, death only shall separate us'. And they urged so much to go with him, that he ceased speaking to them; and they went after him and would not return; And when the kings returned they caused a census to be taken, in order to know the number of remaining men that went with Enoch; and it was upon the seventh day that Enoch ascended into heaven in a whirlwind, with horses and chariots of fire [2 Kings 2:11]. And on the eighth day all the kings that had been with Enoch sent to bring back the number of men that were with Enoch, in that place from which he ascended into heaven. And all those kings went to the place and they found the earth there filled with snow, and upon the snow were large stones of snow, and one said to the other, 'Come, let us break through the snow and see, perhaps the men that remained with Enoch are dead, and are now under the stones of snow', and they searched but could not find him, for he had ascended into heaven [2 Kings 2:1–25]. [11] (Johnson, *Jasher*, 11–12)

When Enoch had talked to the people, the Lord sent out darkness on to the earth, and there was darkness, and it covered those men standing with Enoch, and they took Enoch up on to the highest heaven, where the Lord is. And there God received him and placed him before His face, and the darkness went off from the earth, and light came again. And the people saw and did not understand how Enoch had been taken, and they glorified God, and found a scroll in which was written 'The God of the Spiritual'. Then all went to their dwelling places…He was taken up to heaven…He wrote all these signs of all creation, which the Lord created, and wrote three hundred and sixty-six books, and handed them over to his sons…and was again taken up to heaven…As every man's nature in this life is dark [Jeremiah 17:9–10], so are also his conception, birth, and departure from this life…Methuselah and his brethren, all the sons of Enoch, made haste, and erected an altar at that place called Achuzan, where Enoch had been taken up to heaven. And they took sacrificial oxen and summoned all people and sacrificed the sacrifice before the Lord's face. All people, the elders of the people and the whole assembly came to the feast and brought gifts to the sons of Enoch. And they made a great feast, rejoicing and making merry three days, praising God, who had given them such a sign through Enoch, who had found favor with Him, and that they should hand it on to their sons from generation to generation, from age to age. Amen.[12] (Lumpkin, *Enoch*, 284–285)

If there is a Mount Rushmore of faith, then Enoch would be on it. Hebrews 11:5–6 states, "By faith Enoch was taken away so that he did not see death, 'and was not found, because God had taken him'; for before he was taken he had this testimony, that he pleased God. But without faith it is impossible to please Him, for he who comes to God must believe that He is, and that He is a rewarder of those who diligently seek Him."

The Prayer of Enoch

Enoch also knew of the coming deluge and this was his prayer:

> And I lifted up my hands in righteousness and blessed the Holy and Great One, and spoke with the breath of my mouth, and with the tongue of flesh, which God has made for the children of the flesh of men, that they should speak therewith, and He gave them breath and a tongue and a mouth that they should speak therewith: Blessed be You, O Lord, King, Great and mighty in your greatness, Lord of the whole creation of heaven, King of kings and God of the whole world [Psalm 8]. And Your power and kingship and greatness abide for ever and ever, and throughout all generations Your dominion and all heavens are Your throne for ever, and the whole earth your footstool for ever and ever [Isaiah 66:1]. For You have made and You rule all things, and nothing is too hard for You, wisdom never departs from the place of Your throne, nor turns away from Your presence [Proverbs 1, 2, and 4]. You know and see and hear everything, and there is nothing hidden from You for You see everything. And now the angels of Your heavens are guilty of trespass, and on the flesh of men abide Your wrath until the great day of judgment. And now, O God and Lord and Great King, I implore and beseech You to fulfill my prayer, to leave me a posterity on earth, and not destroy all the flesh of man, and make the earth without inhabitant, so that there should be an eternal destruction. And now, my Lord, destroy from the earth the flesh which has aroused Your wrath, but the flesh of righteousness and uprightness establish as an eternal plant bearing seed for ever, and hide not Your face from

the prayer of Your servant, O lord.[13] (Lumpkin, *Enoch*, 151–153)

His prayer would be answered in the coming deluge and with his great-grandson Noah and the building of the ark.

Also, I would ask that you read the prayer of Abraham [Genesis 18:16–33], the prayers of Jacob [Genesis 28:20–22 and 32:9–12], the prayer of David [1 Chronicles 29:10–20], the prayer of Solomon [2 Chronicles 6:12–42], and finally, the prayer of Jesus found in John 17:1–26:

"Jesus spoke these words, lifted up His eyes to heaven, and said: 'Father, the hour has come. Glorify Your Son, that Your Son also may glorify You, as You have given Him authority over all flesh, that He should give eternal life to as many as You have given Him. And this is eternal life, that they may know You, the only true God, and Jesus Christ whom You have sent. I have glorified You on the earth. I have finished the work which You have given Me to do. And now, O Father, glorify Me together with Yourself, with the glory which I had with You before the world was. I have manifested Your name to the men whom You have given Me out of the world. They were Yours, You gave them to Me, and they have kept Your word. Now they have known that all things which You have given Me are from You. For I have given to them the words which You have given Me; and they have received them, and have known surely that I came forth from You; and they have believed that You sent Me. I pray for them. I do not pray for the world but for those whom You have given Me, for they are Yours. And all Mine are Yours, and Yours are Mine, and I am glorified in them. Now I am no longer in the world, and I come to You. Holy Father, keep through Your name those whom You have given Me, that they may be one as We are. While I was with them in the world, I kept them in Your name. Those whom You gave Me I have kept; and none of them is lost except the son of perdition, that the Scripture might be fulfilled. But now I come to You, and these things I speak in the world, that they may have My joy fulfilled in themselves. I have given them Your word; and the world has hated them because they are not of the world, just as I am not of the world. I do not pray that You should take them out of the world, but that You should keep them from the evil one. They are not of the world, just as I am not of the world. Sanctify them by Your truth. Your word is truth. As You sent Me into the world, I also have sent them into the world. And for their sakes I sanctify Myself, that they also may be sanctified by the truth. I do not pray for these alone, but also for those who will believe in Me through their word; that they all may be one, as You, Father, are in Me, and I in You; that they also may be one in Us, that the world may believe that You sent Me. And the glory which You gave Me I have given them, that they may be one just as We are one: I in them, and You in Me; that they may be made perfect in one, and that the world may know that You have sent Me, and have loved them as You have loved Me. Father, I desire that they also whom You gave Me may be with Me where I am, that they may behold My glory which You have given Me; for You loved Me before the foundation of the world. O righteous Father! The world has not known You, but I have known You; and these have known that You sent Me. And I have declared to them Your name, and will declare it, that the love with which You loved Me may be in them, and I in them'." (NKJV)

Appendix A

Adam to the Great Flood

AE = After Eden   YO = Years Old

	0	1	2	3	4	5	6	7	8	9	10	11	12	13	14	15	16	17
ADAM(930 YO)										930 AE								
SETH(912 YO)		130 AE									1042 AE							
ENOS(H)(905 YO)			235 AE									1140 AE						
CAINAN(910 YO)				325 AE									1235 AE					
MAHALALEL(895 YO)				395 AE									1290 AE					
JARED(962 YO)					460 AE										1422 AE			
ENOCH(365 YO)							622 AE			987 AE								
METHUSELAH(969 YO)							687 AE										1656 AE	
LAMECH(777 YO)									874 AE								1651 AE	
NOAH(600 YO @ Flood)											1056 AE						1656	
HUNDREDS (AE)	**0**	**1**	**2**	**3**	**4**	**5**	**6**	**7**	**8**	**9**	**10**	**11**	**12**	**13**	**14**	**15**	**16**	**17**

1656 AE = The Flood

The Fallen Angels & Their Teachings

Genesis 6:1–2, and 4 states, "Now it came to pass, when men began to multiply on the face of the earth, and daughters were born to them, that the sons of God saw the daughters of men, that they were beautiful; and they took wives for themselves of all whom they chose…There were giants on the earth in those days, and also afterward, when the sons of God came into the daughters of men and they bore children to them. Those were the mighty men who were of old, men of renown." And Jude 1:6 says, "And the angels who did not keep their proper domain, but left their own abode, He has reserved in everlasting chains under darkness for the judgment of the great day."

One of the main things that Enoch did was become an intercessor for the angels who fell, and God. He talks about what they did when they fell to earth:

> And the angels, the sons of heaven, saw and lusted after them [Genesis 6:2], and said to one another: 'Come, let us choose us wives from among the children of men and have children with them'. And Semjaza, who was their leader, said to them: 'I fear you will not agree to do this deed, and I alone shall have to pay the penalty of this great sin'. And they all answered him and said: 'Let us all swear an oath, and all bind ourselves by mutual curses so we will not abandon this plan but to do this thing'. Then they all swore together and bound themselves by mutual curses. And they were in all two hundred who descended in the days of Jared in the summit of Mount Hermon, and they called it Mount Hermon, because they had sworn and bound themselves by mutual curses on the act…And all of them together went and took wives for themselves, each choosing one for himself, and they began to go in to them and to defile themselves with sex with them [Genesis 6:1–2, 4], and the angels taught them charms and spells, and the cutting of roots, and made them acquainted with plants. And the women became

pregnant, and they bare large giants [Genesis 6:4], whose height was three thousand cubits (4500 feet). The giants consumed all the work and toil of men. And when men could no longer sustain them, the giants turned against them and devoured mankind. And they began to sin against birds, and beasts, and reptiles, and fish, and to devour one another's flesh, and drank the blood [Leviticus 19:26]. Then the earth laid accusation against the lawless ones. And Azazel taught men to make swords, and knives, and shields, and breastplates, and taught them about metals of the earth [Genesis 4:22] and the art of working them, and bracelets, and ornaments, and the use of antimony, and the beautifying of the eyelids, and all kinds of precious stones, and all coloring and dyes. And there was great impiety, they turned away from God, and committed fornication, and they were led astray, and became corrupt in all their ways [Genesis 6:11–12]. Semjaza taught the casting of spells, and root-cuttings, Armaros taught counter-spells, Baraqijal taught astrology, Kokabel taught the constellations, Ezeqeel the knowledge of the clouds, Araqiel the signs of the earth, Shamsiel the signs of the sun, and Sariel the course of the moon. And as men perished, they cried, and their cry went up to heaven.[14] (Lumpkin, *Enoch*, 26–30)

The depravity of mankind, which began to show itself in the time of Enosh, had increased monstrously in the time of his grandson Jared, by reason of the fallen angels… Two hundred angels descended to the summit of Mount Hermon, which owes its name to this very occurrence… Under the leadership of twenty captains they defiled themselves with the daughters of men, unto whom they taught charms, conjuring formulas, how to cut roots, and the efficacy of plants. The issue from these mixed marriages was a race of giants [Genesis 6:4], three thousand ells (4500 feet) tall, who consumed the possessions of men. When all had vanished, and they could obtain nothing more from them, the giants turned against men and devoured many of them, and the remnant of men began to trespass against the birds, beasts, reptiles, and fishes, eating their flesh and drinking their blood [Deuteronomy 12:23–25]...While all these abominations defiled the earth, the pious Enoch lived in a secret place. None among men knew his abode, or what had become of him, for he was sojourning with the angel watchers and holy ones.[15] (Ginzberg, *Legends*, 45)

I do not necessarily believe that the giants were 4,500 feet tall, but they were definitely humungous. It could possibly be a mistranslation of Enoch from the original version. It is my belief that these are the ones who built every megalithic and monolithic site on earth. There is entirely no way that human beings our size built these places, the stones are just too big (some weighing 200 tons as is the case at Baalbek Temple in present day Lebanon). Our machines today cannot even lift stones that big. Now, an angel with sophisticated technology and giants could easily do this. Some of these sites have precision cuts in the stones (Puma Punku in present day Peru, the Great Pyramids of Egypt are just two examples). We are told by mainstream archaeology and history that our ancestors were hunters and gatherers with stone tools, but I believe they were much more intelligent thanks to the fallen angels. Were these stones actually cut with some sort of tool? Were they melted to an exact fit (fabricated)? Nobody really knows why, how, or who built these sites, but someone or something did, and it is my belief the fallen angels and their giant children, with the help of our ancestors at the time, built all of these sites. This is completely plausible if we understand that the earth, dry land, was at one time in the distant past all connected as one land.

The giants born to the angels are not the same giants that lived after the flood. As stated in the chapter on Adam and Eve, humans were bigger before the flood. An earthly woman that gets impregnated by an angel does not receive that angels' genes, however the child does. The giants born to these angels did not impregnate earthly women, so they did not pass their giant genetics onto mankind.

Read the report of giants in the land the Israelites were to settle in brought back to Moses found in Numbers 13:31–33: "But the men who had gone up with him said, 'We are not able to up against the people, for they are stronger than we'. And they gave the children of Israel a bad report of the land which they had spied out, saying, 'The land through which we have gone as spies is a land that devours its inhabitants, and all the people whom we saw in it are men of great stature. There we saw giants (the descendants of Anak came from the giants); and we were like grasshoppers in our own sight, and so we were in their sight'." Again, in 1 Samuel 17:4–7 it says, "And a champion went out from the camp of the Philistines, named Goliath, whose height was six cubits and a span (roughly 10 feet tall). He had a bronze helmet on his head, and he was armed with a coat of mail, and the weight of the coat was five thousand shekels of bronze (roughly 123 pounds). And he had bronze armor on his legs and a bronze javelin between his shoulders. Now the staff of his spear was like a weaver's beam, and his iron spearhead weighed six hundred shekels (roughly 15 pounds) …" [1 Chronicles 20:4–8]. Goliath was a big man probably weighing upwards of seven hundred pounds and immensely powerful. Now if he was that big and powerful then the pre-flood giants, and our pre-flood ancestors, were even bigger and more powerful.

Here is an account from Noah:

> 'A command has gone out from the presence of the Lord concerning those who dwell on the earth that their ruin is accomplished because they have learned all the secrets of the angels, and all the violence [Genesis 6:11] of the satans; and all their powers – the most secret ones – and all the power of those who practice sorcery, and the power of witchcraft [Leviticus 19:31, 20:6, and 2 Chronicles 33:6], and the power of those who make molten images for the whole earth. And how silver is produced from the dust of the earth, and how soft metal originates in the earth'…And after that my grandfather Enoch took hold of me by my hand and lifted me up, and said to me: 'Go, for I have asked the Lord of spirits about this disturbance on the earth. And He said to me: 'Because of their unrighteousness their judgment has been determined

and shall not be withheld by Me for ever. Because of the sorceries which they have searched out and learned, the earth and those who dwell on it shall be destroyed'. And from these, they have no place of repentance for ever, because they have shown them what is hidden, and they are the damned. But as for you, my son, the Lord of spirits knows that you are pure and guiltless of this reproach concerning the secrets. And He has destined your name to be among the holy, and will preserve you among those who dwell on the earth; and has destined your righteous seed both for kingship and for great honors, and from your seed shall proceed a fountain of the righteous and holy without number for ever' [Genesis 6:9–13, 7:1, and 8:15–19].[16] (Lumpkin, *Enoch*, 108–110)

So, we just read what the angels who came from heaven taught mankind. It is my belief that they taught the women first, following in the footsteps, so to speak, of their general satan. It was Eve who was deceived first and then Adam through Eve. 1 Timothy 2:14 says, "And Adam was not deceived, but the woman being deceived, fell into transgression." I believe that satan knew the man would listen to the woman, his helper (there is also, what I believe to be, a little-known prophecy about this which I will discuss in further detail in the chapter on Jesus). They taught them how to melt gold, silver, and the like, as well as how to use certain plants for sorcery. They taught humans things only known in heaven and they corrupted the entire earth. Is it any wonder why God would send the deluge?

Their Reprimand & Reasons for the Flood

The angels and their children defiled all things of God and He would punish them for eternity:

And against the angels whom He had sent upon the earth, He was exceedingly wroth, and He gave commandment to root them out of all their dominion, and He bade us to bind them in the depths of the earth [Jude 1:6], and behold they are bound in the midst of them, and are kept separate. And against their sons went forth a command from before His face that they should be smitten with the sword, and be removed from under heaven…And He sent His sword [Hebrews 4:12] into their midst that each should slay his neighbor, and they began to slay each other till they all fell by the sword and were destroyed from the earth [Ezekiel 38:18–23]. And their fathers were witnesses of their destruction, and after this they were bound in the depths of the earth for ever, until the day of the great condemnation when judgment is executed [Jude 1:6] on all those who have corrupted their ways and their works before the Lord.[17] (Johnson, *Jubilees*, 28)

These fallen angels, or 'Ancient Aliens' if you are to believe the show that comes on the History channel, are not, I repeat, not coming back because they are already here, buried under the earth until the day of destruction and judgment.

The sons of God knew who Enoch was and that he had a direct path to God so they ask Enoch to go before God and petition Him on their behalf:

And they asked me to write a petition for them that they might find forgiveness, and to read their petition in the presence of the Lord of heaven. They had been forbidden to speak with Him nor were they to lift up their eyes to heaven for shame of their sins because they had been condemned. Then I wrote out their petition, and the prayer in regard to their spirits and their deeds individually and in regard to their requests that they should obtain forgiveness and forbearance…This is the book of the words of righteousness, and of the reprimand of the eternal Watchers in accordance with the command of the holy great ones in that vision I saw in my sleep. What I will now say with a tongue of flesh and with the breath of my mouth: which the Great One has given to men to speak with it and to understand with the hearts. As He has created and given to man the power of understanding the word of wisdom, so has He created me also and given me the power of reprimanding the Watchers, the children of heaven. I wrote out your petition, and in my vision it appeared that your petition will not be granted to you throughout all the days of eternity, and that judgment has been finally passed on you [Jude 1:6]: Your petition will not be granted. From here on you shall not ascend into heaven again for all eternity, and you will be bound on earth for all eternity. Before this you will see the destruction of your beloved sons and you shall have no pleasure in them, but they shall fall before you by the sword. Your petition shall not be granted on their behalf or on yours, even though you weep and pray and speak all the words contained in my writings.[18] (Lumpkin, *Enoch*, 39–41).

God would then send Enoch back to the fallen:

And He answered and said to me, and I heard His voice: 'Do not be afraid, Enoch, you righteous man and scribe of righteousness. Approach and hear My voice. Go and say to the Watchers of heaven, for whom you have come to intercede: 'You should intercede for men, and not men for you. Why and for what cause have you left the high, holy, and eternal heaven, and had sex with women, and defiled yourselves with the daughters of men and taken to yourselves wives, and done like the children of earth, and begotten giants as your sons? Though you were holy, spiritual, living the eternal life, you have defiled yourselves with the blood of women, and have begotten children with the blood of flesh, and, as the children of men, you have lusted after flesh and blood like those who die and are killed. This is why I have given men wives, that they might impregnate them, and have children by them, that deeds might continue on the earth. But you were formerly spiritual, living the eternal life, and immortal for all generations of the world. Therefore I have not appointed wives for you; you are spiritual beings of heaven, and in heaven was your dwelling place' [Luke 20:34]. And now, the giants, who are produced from the spirits and flesh, shall be called evil spirits on the earth [Ephesians 6:12], and shall live on the earth. Evil spirits have come out from their bodies because they are born from men and from the holy Watchers, their beginning is of primal origin; …And the spirits of the giants afflict, oppress, destroy, attack, war, destroy, and cause trouble on the earth [Revelation 16:14]. They take no food, but do not hunger or thirst. They cause offences but are not observed. And these spirits shall rise up against the children of men and against the women, because they have proceeded from them in the days of the slaughter and destruction. And at the death of the giants, spirits will go out and shall destroy [Deuteronomy 18:9–14] without incurring judgment, coming from their bodies, their flesh shall be destroyed until the day of the consummation, the great judgment in which the age shall be consummated, over the Watchers and the godless, and shall be wholly consummated. And now as to the Watchers who have sent you to intercede for them, who had been in heaven before, say to them: 'You were in heaven, but all the mysteries of heaven had not been revealed to you, and you knew worthless ones, and these in the hardness of your hearts you have made known to the women, and through these mysteries women and men work much evil on the earth'. Say to them therefore: 'You have no peace'.[19] (Lumpkin, *Enoch*, 44–47)

So, the evil spirits, or demons, came from the giant children of the fallen angels, and this makes complete sense being that they were half human and half angel. And they know who Jesus is! Matthew 8:28–32 states, "When He had come to the other side, to the country of the

Gergesenes, there met Him two demon-possessed men, coming out of the tombs, exceedingly fierce, so that no one could pass that way. And suddenly they cried out, saying, 'What have we to do with You, Jesus, You Son of God? Have You come to torment us before the time?' Now a good way off from them there was a herd of many swine feeding. So the demons begged Him, saying, 'If You cast us out, permit us to go away into the herd of swine.' And He said to them, 'Go.' So when they had come out, they went into the herd of swine. And suddenly the whole herd of swine ran violently down the steep place into the sea, and perished in the water" [Mark 5:1–13 and Luke 8:26–33]. Again, we read in Mark 1:21–27, "Then they went to Capernaum, and immediately on the Sabbath Hen entered the synagogue and taught. And they were astonished at His teaching, for He taught them as one having authority, and not as the scribes. Now there was a man in their synagogue with an unclean spirit. And he cried out, saying, 'Let us alone! What have we to do with You, Jesus of Nazareth? Did You come to destroy us? I know who You are – the Holy One of God!' But Jesus rebuked him, saying, 'Be quiet, and come out of him!' And when the unclean spirit had convulsed him and cried out with a loud voice, he came out of him. Then they were all amazed, so that they questioned among themselves, saying, 'What is this? What new doctrine is this? For with authority He commands even the unclean spirits, and they obey Him'" [Luke 4:31–37].

Here is an account of how God dealt with these transgressors from heaven:

> And then Michael, Uriel, Raphael, and Gabriel looked down from heaven and saw much blood being shed on the earth, and all lawlessness being done on the earth... And they said to the Lord of the ages: 'Lord of lords, God of gods, King of kings, and God of the ages, the throne of your glory endures through all the generations of the ages, and your name holy and glorious and blessed to all the ages! You have made all things, and you have power over all things: and all things are revealed and open in your sight, and you see all things, and nothing can hide itself from you [Hebrews 4:13]. Look at what Azazel has

done, who hath taught all unrighteousness on earth and revealed the eternal secrets which were made and kept in heaven, which men were striving to learn: And Semjaza, who taught spells, to whom you gave authority to rule over his associates. And they have gone to the daughters of men on the earth, and have had sex with the women, and have defiled themselves, and revealed to them all kinds of sins. And the women have borne giants [Genesis 6:4], and the whole earth has thereby been filled with blood and unrighteousness' [Genesis 6:11–12]...Then said the Most High, the Great and Holy One, 'Uriel, go to the son of Lamech. Say to him: '...Hide yourself!' and reveal to him the end that is approaching: that the whole earth will be destroyed, and a flood is about to come on the whole earth, and will destroy everything on it. And now instruct him as to what he must do to escape that his offspring may be preserved for all generations of the world' [Genesis 6:13–14]. And again the Lord dais to Raphael: 'Bind Azazel hand and foot, and cast him into darkness and split open the desert, which is in Dudael, and cast him in. And fill the hole by covering him rough and jagged rocks, and cover him with darkness, and let him live there for ever, and cover his face that he may not see the light. And on the day of the great judgment he shall be hurled into the fire' [Jude 1:5]...To Gabriel said the Lord: 'Proceed against the bastards and the reprobates, and against the children of fornication and destroy the children of fornication and the children of the Watchers. Cause them to go against one another that they may destroy each other in battle: shorten their days'...And the Lord said to Michael: 'Go, bind Semjaza and his team who have associated with women, and have defiled themselves in all their uncleanness. When their sons have slain one another, and they have seen the destruction of their beloved ones, bind them fast for seventy generations under the hills of the earth, until the day of the consummation of their judgment and until the eternal judgment is accomplished. In those days they shall be led off to the abyss of fire and to the torment and the prison in which they shall be confined for ever'.[20] (Lumpkin, *Enoch*, 30–35)

God sends His Sword amongst the giants and they end up fighting and killing each other, and their fathers, the angels, witness this before they are thrown into darkness.

The Sword of God could either mean the archangel Michael, the archangel Uriel, or it could mean Jesus, His Son. In some legends it is Uriel who stands at the gate of Eden with a fiery sword. Daniel 10:10 – 11:1 states:

> "Suddenly, a hand touched me, which made me tremble on my knees and on the palms of my hands. And he said to me, 'O Daniel, man greatly beloved, understand the words that I speak to you, and stand upright, for I have now been sent to you.' While he was speaking this word to me, I stood trembling. Then he said to me, 'Do not fear, Daniel, for from the first day that you set your heart to understand, and to humble yourself before your God, your words were heard; and I have come because of your words. But the prince of the kingdom of Persia withstood me twenty-one days; and behold, Michael, one of the chief princes, came to help me, for I had been left alone there with the kings of Persia. Now I have come to make you understand what will happen to your people in the latter days, for the vision refers to many days yet to come.' When he had spoken such words to me, I turned my face towards the ground and became speechless. And suddenly, *one* (Jesus) having the likeness of the sons of men touched my lips; then I opened my mouth and spoke, saying to him who stood before me, 'My lord, because of the vision my sorrows have overwhelmed me, and I have retained no strength. For how can this servant of my lord talk with you, my lord? As for me, no strength remains in me now,

nor is any breath left in me.' Then again, the *one* (Jesus) having the likeness of a man touched me and strengthened me. And he said, 'O man greatly beloved, fear not! Peace be to you; be strong, yes, be strong!' So when he spoke to me I was strengthened, and said, 'Let my lord speak, for you have strengthened me.' Then he said, 'Do you know why I have come to you? And now I must return to fight with the prince of Persia; and when I have gone forth, indeed the prince of Greece will come. But I will tell you what is noted in the Scripture of Truth. (No one upholds me against these, except Michael your prince. Also in the first year of Darius the Mede, I, even I, stood up to confirm and strengthen him)." (NKJV)

It is my belief that the '*one*' mentioned here is Jesus Himself, and that the 'prince' of these kingdoms mentioned is satan in a spiritual sense, but we also know that in the physical sense the 'prince' of Greece refers to Alexander the Great. Michael is also seen as the protector of the Israelites. We can also read in Jude verse 9, "Yet Michael the archangel, in contending with the devil, when he disputed about the body of Moses, dared not bring against him a reviling accusation, but said, 'The Lord rebuke you!'"

I believe that this Sword of God is actually Jesus Himself due to what we find written in Hebrews 4:11–13, "Let us therefore be diligent to enter that rest, lest anyone fall according to the same example of disobedience. For the word of God is living and powerful, and sharper than any two-edged sword, piercing even to the division of soul and spirit, and of joints and marrow, and is a discerner of the thoughts and intents of the heart. And there is no creature hidden from His sight, but all things are naked and open to the eyes of Him to whom we must give account." I will leave it up to the reader to decide for themselves who or what this Sword of God is.

Enoch also sees the equipment being made for those angels:

And there my eyes saw how they made their instruments for them, iron chains [Jude 1:6] of immeasurable weight. And I asked the angel of peace who was with me, saying: 'For whom are these chains being prepared?' And he aid to me: 'These are being prepared for the hosts of Azazel, so that they may take them and throw them into the bottom of the pit of hell, and they shall cover their jaws with rough stones as the Lord of spirits commanded. And Michael, and Gabriel, and Raphael, and Phanuel shall take hold of them on that great day, and throw them into the burning furnace on that day, that the Lord of spirits may take vengeance on them for their unrighteousness in becoming servants to satan and for leading astray those who live on the earth'. And in those days punishment will come from the Lord of spirits, and He will open all the storehouses of waters above heavens [Genesis 7:11], and of the fountains which are under the surface of the earth.[21] (Lumpkin, *Enoch*, 88–89)

So, the giant children were killed. The sinners from heaven who chose to follow satan are reserved in darkness for the day of judgment.

The flood happened because the men of that generation harkened to satan and his followers instead of their Creator, God. "And everyone sold himself to work iniquity and to shed much blood, and the earth was filled with iniquity. And after this they sinned against the beasts and birds, and all that moveth and walketh on the earth: and much blood was shed on the earth, and every imagination and desire of men imagined vanity and evil continually [Genesis 6:5, 11–12]. And the Lord destroyed everything from off the face of the earth; because of the wickedness of their deeds, and because of the blood which they had shed in the midst of the earth He destroyed everything."[22] However, there was one man who was righteous and God would start anew with him and his children. "...Noah followed in the ways of his grandfather Methuselah, while all other men of the time rose up against this pious king. So far from observing his precepts, they pursued the evil inclination of their hearts, and perpetrated all sorts of abominable deeds. Chiefly the fallen angels and their giant posterity caused the depravity of mankind. The blood spilled by the giants cried unto heaven from the ground, and the four archangels accused the fallen angels and their sons before God..."[23]

All of the fallen angels are waiting for their appointed time, or the Day of the Lord. Revelation 9:13–15 says, "Then the sixth angel sounded: And I heard a voice from the four horns of the golden altar which is before God, saying to the sixth angel who had the trumpet, 'Release the four angels who are bound at the great river Euphrates'. So the four angels, who had been prepared for the hour and day and month and year, were released to kill a third of mankind."

The Legend of Metatron

There is a legend about Enoch and what became of him after his ascension:

> Before Enoch could be admitted to service near the Divine Throne, the gates of wisdom were opened unto him, and the gates of understanding, and of discernment, of life, peace, and the Shekinah, of strength and power, of might, loveliness, and grace, of humility and fear of sin. Equipped by God with extraordinary wisdom, sagacity, judgment, knowledge, learning, compassionateness, love, kindness, grace, humility, strength, power, might, splendor, beauty, shapeliness, and all other excellent qualities [Galatians 5:22–23], beyond the endowment of any of the celestial beings, Enoch received, besides, many thousand blessings from God, and his height and his breadth became equal to the height and the breadth of the world, and thirty-six wings were attached to his body, to the right and to the left, each as large as the world, and three hundred and sixty-five thousand eyes were bestowed upon him, each brilliant as the sun. A magnificent throne was erected for him beside the gates of the seventh celestial palace, and a herald proclaimed throughout the heavens concerning him, who was henceforth to be called Metatron in the celestial regions: 'I have appointed My servant Metatron as prince and chief over all the princes in My realm... Whatever angel has a request to prefer to Me, shall appear before Metatron, and what he will command at

My bidding, ye must observe and do, for the prince of wisdom and the prince of understanding are at his service, and they will reveal unto him the sciences of the celestials and terrestrials, the knowledge of the present order of the world and the knowledge of the future order of the world'...Out of the love He bore Enoch, God arrayed him in a magnificent garment, to which every kind of luminary in existence was attached, and a crown gleaming with forty-nine jewels, the splendor of which pierced to all parts of the seven heavens and to the four corners of the earth. In the presence of the heavenly family, He set this crown upon the head of Enoch, and called him 'the little Lord'. It bears also the letters by means of which heaven and earth were created, and seas and rivers, mountains and valleys, planets and constellations, lightning and thunder, snow and hail, storm and whirlwind – these and also all things needed in the world, and the mysteries of creation. Even the princes of the heavens, when they see Metatron, tremble before him, and prostrate themselves... When Enoch was transformed into Metatron, his body was turned into celestial fire – his flesh became flame, his veins fire, his bones glimmering coals, the light of his eyes heavenly brightness, his eyeballs torches of fire, his hair a flaring blaze, all his limbs and organs burning sparks, and his frame a consuming fire. To right of him sparkled flames of fire, to left of him burnt torches of fire, and on all sides he was engirdled by storm and whirlwind, hurricane and thundering.[24] (Ginzberg, *Legends*, 49–50)

Noah & the Great Flood

"This is the genealogy of Noah. Noah was a just man, perfect in his generations. Noah walked with God. And Noah begot three sons: Shem, Ham, and Japheth." [Genesis 6:9–10]

"Then the Lord saw that the wickedness of man was great in the earth, and that every intent of the thoughts of his heart was only evil continually. And the Lord was sorry the He had made man on the earth, and He was grieved in His heart. So the Lord said 'I will destroy man whom I have created from the face of the earth, both man and beast, creeping things and birds of the air, for I am sorry that I have made them.' But Noah found grace in the eyes of the Lord." [Genesis 6:5–8]

"But as the days of Noah were, so also will the coming of the Son of Man be. For as in the days before the flood, they were eating and drinking, marrying and giving in marriage, until the day that Noah entered the ark, and did not know until the flood came and took them all away, so also will the coming of the Son of Man be." [Matthew 24:37–39]

"The earth was also corrupt before God, and the earth was filled with violence. So God looked upon the earth, and indeed it was corrupt; for all flesh had corrupted their way on the earth. And God said to Noah, 'The end of all flesh has come before Me, for the earth is filled with violence through them; and behold, I will destroy them with the earth. Make yourself an ark of gopher wood…And behold, I Myself and bringing floodwaters on the earth, to destroy from under heaven all flesh in which is the breath of life; everything that is on the earth shall die'. " [Genesis 6:11–14, 17]

"By faith Noah, being divinely warned of things not yet seen, moved with godly fear, prepared an ark for the saving of his household, by which he condemned the world and became heir of the righteousness which is according to faith." [Hebrews 11: 7]

"And did not spare the ancient world, but saved Noah, one of eight people, a preacher of righteousness, bringing in the flood on the world of the ungodly." [2 Peter 2:5]

The Just Man

Why Noah? Why not someone else? It is because he was the only righteous man on earth at this time that followed the ways of God taught by his great-grandfather Enoch and passed down through his grandfather Methuselah and his father Lamech [Genesis 6:9]. A couple of accounts talk about him:

> By the name Noah he was called only by his grandfather Methuselah; his father and all others called him Menahem. His generation was addicted to sorcery, and Methuselah apprehended that his grandson might be bewitched if his true name were known, wherefore he kept it a secret. Menahem, Comforter, suited him as well as Noah [Genesis 5:29]; it indicated that he would be a consoler, if but the evil-doers of his time would repent of their misdeeds...Noah had scarcely come into the world when a marked change was noticeable. Since the curse brought upon the earth by the sin of Adam [Romans 5:12–21], it happened that wheat being sown, yet oats would sprout and grow. This ceased with the appearance of Noah: the earth bore the products planted in it. And it was Noah who, when he was grown to manhood, invented the plough, the scythe, the hoe, and other implements for cultivating the ground. Before him men had worked the land with their bare hands...When God created Adam, He gave him dominion over all things [Genesis 1:26, 28]: the cow obeyed the ploughman, and the furrow was willing to be drawn. But after the fall of Adam all things rebelled against him: the cow refused obedience to the ploughman, and also the furrow was refractory. Noah was born, and all returned to its state preceding the fall of man. Before the birth of Noah, the sea was in the habit of transgressing its bounds twice daily, morning and evening, and flooding the land up to the graves. After his birth it kept within its confines. And the famine that afflicted the world in the time of Lamech, the second of

the ten great famines appointed to come upon it, ceased its ravages with the birth of Noah.[1] (Ginzberg, *Legends*, 51)

And Noah was a just man, he was perfect in his generation [Genesis 6:9], and the Lord chose him to raise up seed from his seed upon the face of the earth [Genesis 10:32]. And the Lord said unto Noah, 'Take unto thee a wife, and beget children, for I have seen thee righteous before Me in this generation [Genesis 7:1]. And thou shalt raise up seed, and thy children with thee, in the midst of the earth'; and Noah went and took a wife, and he chose Naamah the daughter of Enoch, and she was five hundred and eighty years old. And Noah was four hundred and ninety-eight years old, when he took Naamah for a wife. And Naamah conceived and bare a son, and he called his name Japheth, saying, 'God has enlarged me in the earth' [Genesis 9:27]; and she conceived again and bare a son, and he called his name Shem, saying, 'God has made me a remnant, to raise up seed in the midst of the earth'. And Noah was five hundred and two years old when Naamah bare Shem [Genesis 11:10], and the boys grew up and went in the ways of the Lord, in all that Methuselah and Noah their father taught them.[2] (Johnson, *Jasher*, 13–14)

Through Noah, God would show man that He was the Creator and everything listened to Him. It makes perfect sense that Noah would invent tools for working the ground being that he would plant the first garden, or vineyard, after the flood [Genesis 9:20]. We know that these tools make it a little easier to plant and grow the seed of vegetables and sweet-smelling flowers.

The Preacher & The Ark

The flood was coming and Noah knew it because God told him through Enoch, however, God would give the generation more than enough time to stay the flood if they would turn away from their evil ways and follow Him. Genesis 6:3 says, "And the Lord said, 'My Spirit shall not strive with man forever, for he is indeed flesh; yet his days shall be one hundred and twenty years'." A lot of theologians and believers today have not interpreted the verse in the Bible that speaks to this in the correct way. Now it is true that the human life span was shortened drastically after the flood, but people lived over one hundred and twenty years [Genesis 11:10–26]. Abraham died when he was one hundred and seventy-five years old [Genesis 25:7], Isaac died when he was one hundred and eighty years old [Genesis 35:28], Jacob was one hundred and thirty years old when he settled in Egypt [Genesis 47:9], the Negev desert to be exact, and the priest Jehoiada died when he was one hundred and thirty years old [2 Chronicles 24:15]. All of these men lived after the flood and Jehoiada was between two thousand and twenty-five hundred years after the flood.

Noah was allowed to try and get his generation to turn to God and here are some accounts:

> And after the lapse of many years, in the four hundred and eightieth year of the life of Noah, when all those men, who followed the Lord had died away from amongst the sons of men, and only Methuselah was then left, God said unto Noah and Methuselah, saying, ' Speak ye, and proclaim to the sons of men, saying, 'Thus saith the Lord, return from your evil ways and forsake your works', and the Lord will repent of the evil that He declared to do to you, so that it shall not come to pass. For thus saith the Lord, 'Behold I give you a period of one hundred and twenty years [Genesis 6:3]; if you will turn to Me and forsake your evil ways, then will I also turn away from the evil which I told you, and it shall not exist', saith the Lord' [2 Chronicles 7:14]. And Noah and Methuselah spoke all the words of the Lord to the sons of men, day after day, constantly speaking to them. But the sons of men would not hearken to them, nor incline their ears to their words, and they were stiff-necked.[3] (Johnson, *Jasher*, 13)

Even after God had resolved upon the destruction of the sinners, He still permitted His mercy to prevail, in that He sent Noah unto them, who exhorted them for one hundred and twenty years [Genesis 6:3] to amend their ways, always holding the flood over them as a threat. As for them, they but derided him. When they saw him occupying himself with the building of the ark [Genesis 6:13–22] they asked, 'Wherefore this ark?' Noah: 'God will bring a flood upon you." The sinners: 'What sort of flood? If He sends a fire flood, against that we know how to protect ourselves. If it is a flood of waters, then, if the waters bubble up from the earth, we will cover them with iron rods., and if they descend from above, we know a remedy against that, too.' Noah: 'The waters will ooze out from under your feet, and you will not be able to ward them off.' Partly they persisted in their obduracy of heart because Noah had made known to them that the flood would not descend so long as the pious Methuselah sojourned among them. The period of one hundred and twenty years which God had appointed as the term of their probation having expired, Methuselah died, but out of regard for the memory of this pious man God gave them another week's respite [Genesis 7:4], the week of mourning for him. During this time of grace, the laws of nature were suspended, the sun rose in the west and set in the east. To the sinners God gave the dainties that await man in the future world, for the purpose of showing them what they were forfeiting. But all this proved unavailing, and, Methuselah and the other pious men of the generation having departed this life, God brought the deluge upon the earth.[4] (Ginzberg, *Legends*, 53)

The words of the prophet Isaiah ring true about the generation of Noah. Isaiah 6:9–10 states, "And He said, 'Go, and tell this people: 'Keep on hearing, but do not understand; keep on seeing, but do not perceive.' Make the heart of this people dull, and their ears heavy, and shut their eyes; lest they see with their eyes, and hear with their ears, and understand with their heart, and return and be healed'." If it were not for Noah, and his grandfather Methuselah for that matter, being a righteous man, God probably would have flooded the earth sooner. And He would not allow any of the seed of Seth, save Noah for purposes of re-populating the earth, to see this destruction. Isn't it fitting that even though the people are being told what will come, they still are rebellious, they still are prideful, and they still choose to do evil? Sound familiar? Jesus Himself says in Matthew 13:13–15, "Therefore I speak to them in parables, because seeing they do not see, and hearing they do not hear, nor do they understand. And in them the prophecy of Isaiah is fulfilled, which says: 'Hearing you will hear and not understand, and seeing you will see and not perceive; for the hearts of this people have grown dull. Their ears are hard of hearing, and their eyes they have closed, lest they should see with their eyes and hear with their ears, lest they should understand with their hearts and turn, so that I should heal them'." As humans we have free will to choose. It is my hope and prayer that the reader will choose to follow the One God, through His Son Jesus Christ, who created you and loves you unconditionally.

After many years of preaching to the generation God finally tells Noah that the time has come and gives him instructions on how to escape and survive the coming catastrophe. Genesis 6:13–17 states, "And God said to Noah, 'The end of all flesh has come before Me, for the earth is filled with violence through them; and behold, I will destroy them with the earth. Make yourself an ark of gopherwood; make rooms in the ark, and cover it inside and outside with pitch. And this is how you shall make it: The length of the ark shall be three hundred cubits (450 feet), its width fifty cubits (75 feet), and its height thirty cubits (45 feet). You shall make a window for the ark, and you shall finish it to a cubit (1 ½ feet) from above; and set the door of the ark in its side. You shall make it with lower, second, and third decks. And behold, I Myself am bringing floodwaters on the earth, to destroy from under heaven all flesh in which is the breath of life; everything that is on the earth shall die'." Here is a separate report of this:

> 'And behold I will bring the flood waters upon the earth,
> and all flesh be destroyed, from under the heavens all that
> is upon earth shall perish [Genesis 6:17]. And thou and
> thy household shall go and gather two couple of all living

things, male and female, and shall bring them to the ark, to raise up seed from them upon earth. And gather unto thee all food that is eaten by all the animals, that there may be food for thee and them [Genesis 6:19–21]. And thou shalt choose for thy sons three maidens, from the daughters of men, and they shall be wives to thy sons' [Genesis 7:13]…In his five hundred and ninety-fifth year Noah commenced to make the ark, and he made the ark in five years, as the Lord had commanded. Then Noah took the three daughters of Eliakim, son of Methuselah, for wives for his sons, as the Lord had commanded Noah.[5] (Johnson, *Jasher*, 14)

It took Noah five years to build the ark. Five years of non-stop work so that he and his family, along with the animals, could survive the waters upon the earth.

It was the fallen angels and their giant children that led men and animals to corrupt their ways, hence 'them' in Genesis 6:13.

And every man made unto himself a god, and they robbed and plundered every man his neighbor as well as his relative, and they corrupted the earth, and the earth was filled with violence [Genesis 6:11]. And their judges and rulers went to the daughters of men and took their wives by force from their husbands according to their choice, and the sons of men in those days took from the cattle of the earth, the beasts of the field and the fowls of the air, and taught the mixture of animals of one species with the other, in order therewith to provoke the Lord; and God saw the whole earth and it was corrupt, for all flesh had corrupted its way upon earth, all men and all animals [Genesis 6:12]. And the Lord said, 'I will blot out man that I created from the face of the earth, yea from man to the birds of the air, together with cattle and beasts that are in the field for I repent that I made them' [Genesis 6:7]. And all men who walked in the ways of the Lord, died in those days, before the Lord brought the evil upon man which He had declared, for this was from the Lord, that they should not see the evil which the Lord spoke of concerning the sons of men [Matthew 24:22, Luke 21:36, and Romans 3:10]. And Noah found grace in the sight of the Lord, and the Lord chose him and his children to raise up seed [Genesis 7:1] from them upon the face of the whole earth [Genesis 6:1–8]. [6] (Johnson, *Jasher*, 12–13)

In an earlier chapter, I mentioned that the animals talk to and listen to their Creator. Here is an interesting account of that:

At that time, after the death of Methuselah, the Lord said to Noah, 'Go thou with thy household into the ark [Genesis 7:1]; behold I will gather to thee all the animals of the earth, the beasts of the field and the fowls of the air, and they shall all come and surround the ark. And thou shalt go and seat thyself by the doors of the ark, and all the beasts, the animals, and the fowls, shall assemble and place themselves before thee, and such of them as shall come and crouch before thee, shalt thou take and deliver into the hands of thy sons, who shall bring them to the ark, and all that will stand before thee thou shalt leave'. And the Lord brought this about on the next day, and animals, beasts and fowls came in great multitudes and surround the ark. And Noah went and seated himself by the door of the ark, and of all flesh that crouched before him, he brought into the ark, and all that stood before him he left upon earth. And a lioness came, with her two whelps, male and female, and the three crouched before Noah, and the two whelps rose up against the lioness and smote her, and made her flee from her place, and she went away, and they returned to their places, and crouched upon the earth before Noah. And the lioness ran away, and stood in the place of the lions. And Noah saw this, and wondered greatly, and he rose and took the two whelps, and brought them into the ark.[7] (Johnson, *Jasher*, 14–15)

It is as if the two whelps told their mother she was too old to come along or that they would be better suited to survive being that they would grow strong on the ark. I actually believe that all of the animals that were on the ark were young and not as big as their full-grown counterpart. The animals knew that something drastic was about to happen and God made them come to Noah. The fact that they had to bow to Noah to enter the ark is fascinating. This shows that man does have dominion over all creatures that are on the earth. Genesis 9:1–4 says, "So God blessed Noah and his sons, and said to them: 'Be fruitful and multiply, and fill the earth. And the fear of you and the dread of you shall be on every beast of the earth, on every bird of the air, and on all that move on the earth, and on all the fish of the sea. They are given into your hand. Every moving thing that lives shall be food for you. I have given you all things, even as the green herbs. But you shall not eat flesh with its life, that is, its blood'."

"And lawlessness increased on the earth and all flesh corrupted its way, alike men and cattle and beasts and birds and everything that walketh on the earth – all of them corrupted their ways and their orders, and they began to devour each other, and lawlessness increased on the earth and every imagination of the thoughts of all men was thus evil continually [Genesis 6:5]."[8] The lawlessness spoken of is unrighteousness and the suppressing of the truth; there is a God and He alone is God. Paul writes in Romans 1:18–25:

> "For the wrath of God is revealed from heaven against all ungodliness and unrighteousness of men, who suppress the truth in unrighteousness, because what may be known of God is manifest in them, for God has shown it to them. For since the creation of the world His invisible attributes are clearly seen, being understood by the things that are made, even His eternal power and Godhead, so that they are without excuse, because, although they knew God, they did not glorify Him as God, nor were thankful, but became futile in their thoughts, and their foolish hearts

were darkened. Professing to be wise, they became fools, and changed the glory of the incorruptible God into an image made like corruptible man – and birds and four-footed animals and creeping things. Therefore God also gave them up to uncleanness, in the lusts of their hearts, to dishonor their bodies among themselves, who exchanged the truth of God for the lie, and worshiped and served the creature rather than the Creator, who is blessed forever. Amen." (NKJV)

God allowed a certain number of years (one hundred and twenty to be exact) for man to change his ways. Now, this is going to happen at the end of the age when Jesus comes back for His Church and He gives several parables speaking to this. Jesus says in Matthew 24:32–35, "Now learn this parable from the fig tree: when its branch has already become tender and puts forth leaves, you know that summer is near. So you also, when you see all these things, know that it is near – at the doors! Assuredly, I say to you, this generation will by no means pass away till all these things take place. Heaven and earth will pass away, but My words will by no means pass away." Again, in Matthew 24:46–51, Jesus states, "Who then is a faithful and wise servant, whom his master made ruler over his household, to give them food in due season? Blessed is that servant whom his master, when he comes, will find so doing. Assuredly, I say to you that he will make him ruler over all his goods. But if that evil servant says in his heart, 'My master is delaying his coming', and begins to beat his fellow servants, and to eat and drink with the drunkards, the master of that servant will come on a day when he is not looking for him and at an hour that he is not aware of, and will cut him in two and appoint him his portion with the hypocrites. There shall be weeping and gnashing of teeth." And lastly, Jesus also says in Matthew 25:1–13, "Then the kingdom of heaven shall be likened to ten virgins who took their lamps and went out to meet the bridegroom. Now five of them were wise, and five were foolish. Those who were foolish took their lamps and took no oil with them, but the wise took oil in their vessels with their lamps. But while the bridegroom was delayed, they all slumbered and slept. And at midnight a cry was heard: 'Behold, the bridegroom is coming; go out to meet him!' Then all those virgins arose and trimmed their lamps. And the foolish said to the wise, 'Give us some of your oil, for our lamps are going out.' But the wise answered, saying, 'No, lest there should not be enough for us and you; but go rather to those who sell, and buy for yourselves.' And while they went to buy, the bridegroom came, and those who were ready went in with him to the wedding; and the door was shut. Afterward the other virgins came also, saying, 'Lord, Lord, open to us!' But he answered and said, 'Assuredly, I say to you, I do not know you.' Watch therefore, for you know neither the day nor the hour in which the Son of Man is coming."

Although we do not know the exact time it will happen, we do know what will be happening in the world before [Matthew 24:3–15, Mark 13:3–14, and Luke 21:7–20]. Are you ready? If Jesus came back today would your lamp go out and would you hear the trumpet call? I implore you not to wait until it is too late as those before the flood did. Call on Jesus and He will save you.

The Great Flood

The earth and God's creation were about to go through a remarkable change. It would rain non-stop for forty days and nights [Genesis 7:12]. Not only would it come from above, but the waters of the deep would also spring forth [Genesis 7:11]. This was total annihilation and devastation.

> And on that day, the Lord caused the whole earth to shake, and the sun darkened, and the foundations of the world raged, and the whole earth was moved violently [Revelation 6:12–14], and the lightning flashed, and the thunder roared, and all the fountains in the earth were broken up [Genesis 7:11], such as was not known to the inhabitants before; and God did this mighty act, in order to terrify the sons of men, that there might be no more evil upon earth. And still the sons of men would not return from their evil ways, and they increased the anger of the Lord at that time, and did not even direct their hearts to all this. And at the end of seven days, in the six hundredth year of the life of Noah, the waters of the flood were upon

the earth. And all the fountains of the deep were broken up, and the windows of heaven were opened, and the rain was upon the earth forty days and forty nights…And the sons of men assembled together, about seven hundred thousand men and women, and they came unto Noah to the ark. And they called to Noah, saying, 'Open for us that we may come to thee in the ark – and wherefore shall we die?' And Noah, with a loud voice, answered them from the ark, saying, 'Have you not all rebelled against the Lord, and said that he does not exist? And therefore the Lord brought upon you this evil, to destroy and cut you off from the face of the earth [Genesis 6:7]. Is not this the thing that I spoke to you of one hundred and twenty years back, and you would not hearken to the voice of the Lord, and now do you desire to live upon earth?' And they said to Noah, 'We are ready to return to the Lord; only open for us that we may live and not die'. And Noah answered them, saying, 'Behold now that you see the trouble of your souls, you wish to return to the Lord; why did you not return during these hundred and twenty years [Genesis 6:3], which the Lord granted you as the determined period? But now you come and tell me this on account of the troubles of your souls, now also the Lord will not listen to you, neither will He give ear to you on this day, so that you will not now succeed in you wishes' [Revelation 6:15–16]. And the sons of men approached in order to break into the ark, to come in on account of the rain, for they could not bear the rain upon them. And the Lord sent all the beasts and animals that stood around the ark. And the beasts overpowered them and drove them from that place, and every man went his way and they again scattered themselves upon the face of the earth [Genesis 7:4–24].[9] (Johnson, *Jasher*, 15)

They wanted on board at the last minute. Once they saw the rain and the power of God, they decided they would change their ways. However, it was too late, and they would perish from off the face of the earth. Again, please do not wait until the last minute to call on Jesus.

A major change that took place during the flood and under the water was the division of the lands. Have you ever wondered how the earth was separated into seven different lands or continents today? The flood caused them to begin to separate. I believe in what is known as Pangaea, meaning that at one time in the distant past the earth was one land and connected. Take a look at this account: "And the Lord opened seven flood-gates of heaven, and the mouths of the fountains of the great deep, seven mouths in number. And the flood-gates began to pour down water from the heaven forty days and forty nights [Genesis 7:12], and the fountains of the deep also sent up waters, until the whole world was full of water...and the ark was lift up above the earth [Genesis 7:17-19], and it moved upon the face of the waters...And the ark went and rested on the top of Lubar, one of the mountains of Ararat [Genesis 8:4 and Genesis 7:1–24]."[10] Peleg, one of Noah's descendants through his son Shem, means division. Not only were the people divided via languages, at the Tower of Babel, but the earth was also divided into different lands. Whereas the earth was one land before the flood, after it was multiple lands. The waters of the flood were on the earth for a little over a year [Genesis 7:6 and 8:13–14].

Have you ever seen what a hurricane can do? Can you imagine what it must have been like on the ark during this time? It was very scary for all on board and they probably thought they were not going to make it. Check this out:

> And the ark floated upon the face of the waters, and it was tossed upon the waters so that all the living creatures within were turned about like pottage in a cauldron. And great anxiety seized all the living creatures that were in the ark, and the ark was like to be broken. And all the living creatures that were in the ark were terrified, and the lions roared, and the oxen lowed, and the wolves howled, and every living creature in the ark spoke and lamented in its own language, so that their voices reached to a great distance, and Noah and his sons cried and wept in their troubles; they were greatly afraid that they had reached

the gates of death. And Noah prayed unto the Lord, and cried unto him on account of this, and he said, 'O Lord help us, for we have no strength to bear this evil that has encompassed us, for the waves of the waters have surrounded us, mischievous torrents have terrified us, the snares of death have come before us; answer us, O Lord, answer us, light up thy countenance toward us and be gracious to us, redeem us and deliver us'. And the Lord hearkened to the voice of Noah, and the Lord remembered him [Genesis 8:1]. And a wind passed over the earth, and the waters were still and the ark rested. And the fountains of the deep and the windows of heaven were stopped, and the rain from heaven was restrained [Genesis 8:2]. And the waters decreased in those days, and the ark rested upon the mountains of Ararat [Genesis 8:1–3]. And Noah then opened the windows of the ark, and Noah still called out to the Lord at that time and he said, 'O Lord, who didst form the earth and the heavens and all that are therein, bring forth our souls from this confinement, and from the prison wherein Thou has placed us, for I am much wearied with sighing'. And the Lord hearkened to the voice of Noah, and said to him, 'When thou shalt have completed a full year thou shalt then go forth [Genesis 7 and 8].'[11] (Johnson, *Jasher*, 15–16)

The ark finally comes to rest in what is today northeast Turkey (the actual day that the ark rested is sort of a foreshadowing to the actual day that Jesus would do something as well. More on that in the chapter on Jesus). Noah and his family can leave and start to fulfill their command by God as stated in Genesis 8:15–17, "Then God spoke to Noah, saying, 'Go out of the ark, you and your wife, and your sons and your sons' wives with you. Bring out with you every living thing of all flesh that is with you: birds and cattle and every creeping thing that creeps on the earth, so that they may abound on the earth, and be fruitful and multiply on the earth'."

Here is an account about what happened in the heavens during the flood: "The flood was produced by a union of the male waters, which are above the firmament, and the female waters issuing from the earth. The upper waters rushed through the space left when God removed two stars out of the constellation Pleiades. Afterward, to put a stop to the flood, God had to transfer two stars from the constellation of the Bear to the constellation of the Pleiades. That is why the Bear runs after the Pleiades. She wants her two children back, but they will be restored to her only in the future world. There were other changes among the celestial spheres during the year of the flood. All the time it lasted, the sun and the moon shed no light, whence Noah was called by his name, 'the resting one', for in his life the sun and the moon rested."[12]

See what Job 38:1–33 says:

> "Then the Lord answered Job out of the whirlwind, and said: 'Who is this who darkens counsel by words without knowledge? Now prepare yourself like a man; I will question you, and you shall answer Me. Where were you when I laid the foundations of the earth? Tell Me, if you have understanding. Who determined its measurements? Surely you know! Or who stretched the line upon it? To what were its foundations fastened? Or who laid its cornerstone, when the morning stars sang together, and all the sons of God shouted for joy? Or who shut in the sea with doors, when it burst forth and issued from the womb; when I made the clouds its garment, and thick darkness its swaddling band; when I fixed My limit for it, and set bars and doors; when I said, 'This far you may come, but no farther, and here your proud waves must stop!' Have you commanded the morning since your days began, and caused the dawn to know its place, that it might take hold of the ends of the earth, and the wicked be shaken out of it? It takes on form like clay under a seal, and stands out like a garment. From the wicked their light is withheld, and the upraised arm is broken. Have you entered the springs of the sea? Or have you walked in search of the depths? Have the gates of death been revealed to you? Or have you seen the doors of the shadow of death? Have you

comprehended the breadth of the earth? Tell Me, if you know all this. Where is the way to the dwelling of light? And darkness, where is its place, that you may take it to its territory, that you may know the paths to its home? Do you know it, because you were born then, or because the number of your days is great? Have you entered the treasury of the snow, or have you seen the treasury of hail, which I have reserved for the time of trouble, for the day of battle and war? By what way is light diffused, or the east wind scattered over the earth? Who has divided a channel for the overflowing water, or a path for the thunderbolt, to cause it to rain on a land where there is no one, a wilderness in which there is no man; to satisfy the desolate waste, and cause to spring forth the growth of tender grass? Has the rain a father? Or who has begotten the drops of dew? From whose womb comes the ice? And the frost of heaven, who gives it birth? The waters harden like stone, and the surface of the deep is frozen. Can you bind the cluster of the Pleiades, or loose the belt of Orion? Can you bring out Mazzaroth in its season? Or can you guide the Great Bear with its cubs? Do you know the ordinances of the heavens? Can you set their dominion over the earth?" (NKJV)

Only God knows the answers to all of these questions, and many more throughout chapters 38 and 39 of Job, because He is the Creator.

The Legend of the Birth

And after some days my son Methuselah took a wife for his son, Lamech, and she became pregnant by him and bore a son. And his body was white as snow and red as the blooming of a rose, and the hair of his head and his long curls were white as wool, and his eyes beautiful. And when he opened his eyes, he lit up the whole house like the sun, and the whole house was very bright. And on it he levitated in the hands of the midwife, opened his mouth, and conversed with the Lord of righteousness. And his father, Lamech, was afraid of him and fled, and came to his father Methuselah. And he said to him: 'I have begotten a strange son, different and unlike man, and resembling the sons of the God of heaven; and his nature is different and he is not like us, and his eyes are as the rays of the sun, and his face is glorious. And it seems to me that he did not spring forth from me but from the angels, and I fear that in his days a wonder may be performed on the earth. And now, my father, I am here to ask you and beg you that you may go to Enoch, our father, and learn from him the truth, for his dwelling place is among the angels'. And when Methuselah heard the words of his son, he came to me to the ends of the earth; for he had heard that I was there, and he cried aloud, and I heard his voice and I came to him. And I said to him: 'Behold, here am I, my son, why have you come to me?' And he answered and said: 'Because of a great cause of anxiety have I come to you, and because of a disturbing vision have I approached. And now, my father, hear me. To Lamech, my son, there has been born a son, the like of whom there is none other, and his nature is not like man's nature, and the color of his body is whiter than snow and redder than the bloom of a rose, and the hair of his head is whiter than wool, and his eyes are like the rays of the sun, and he opened his eyes and the whole house lit up. And he levitated in the hands of the midwife, and opened his mouth and blessed the Lord of heaven. And his father Lamech became afraid and fled to me, and did not believe that he was sprung from him, but that he was in the likeness of the angels of heaven; and now I have come to you that you may make known to me the truth'. And I, Enoch, answered and said to him: 'The Lord will do a new thing on the earth, and this I have already seen in a vision, and make known to you that in the generation of my father Jared some of the angels of heaven violated the word of the Lord. And they commit sin and broke the law, and have had sex with women and committed sin with them, and have married some of them, and have had children by them. And they shall produce on the earth giants not according to the spirit, but according to the flesh, and there shall be a great punishment on the earth, and the earth shall be cleansed from all impurity. There shall come a great destruction over the whole earth, and there shall be a flood and a great destruction for one year. And this son who has been born to you shall be left on the earth, and his three children shall be saved with him: when all mankind that are on the earth shall die, he and his sons shall be saved. And now make known to your son, Lamech, that he who has been born is in truth his son, and call his name Noah; for he shall be left to you, and he and his sons shall be saved from the destruction, which shall come on the earth on account of all the sin and all the unrighteousness, which shall be full on the earth in his days. And after that there shall be more unrighteousness than that which was done before on the earth; for I know the mysteries of the holy ones; for He, the Lord, has showed me and informed me, and I have read them in heavenly tablets'.[13] (Lumpkin, *Enoch*, 211–214)

Noah was indeed different, and God would do a new thing on the earth through him and his seed.

Jesus & the Prophecies

"Then God said, 'Let Us make man in Our image, according to Our likeness'..." [Genesis 1:26]

"And I will put enmity between you and the woman, and between your seed and her Seed; He shall bruise your head, and you shall bruise His heel." [Genesis 3:15]

"In the beginning was the Word, and the Word was with God, and the Word was God. He was in the beginning with God. All things were made through Him, and without Him nothing was made that was made. In Him was life, and the life was the light of men. And the light shines in the darkness, and the darkness did not comprehend it." [John 1:1–5]

"Surely He has borne our griefs and carried our sorrows; yet we esteemed Him stricken, smitten by God, and afflicted. But He was wounded for our transgressions, He was bruised for our iniquities; the chastisement for our peace was upon Him, and by His stripes we are healed. All we like sheep have gone astray; we have turned, every one, to his own way; and the Lord has laid on Him the iniquity of us all." [Isaiah 53:4–6...read all of Isaiah 53]

"I am the Alpha and the Omega, the Beginning and the End', says the Lord, 'who is and who was and who is to come, the Almighty." [Revelation 1:8]

"And Jesus came and spoke to them, saying, 'All authority has been given to Me in heaven and on earth. Go therefore and make disciples of all the nations, baptizing them in the name of the Father and of the Son and of the Holy Spirit, teaching them to observe all things that I have commanded you; and lo, I am with you always, even to the end of the age.' Amen." [Matthew 28:18–20]

HIS Name

I mentioned earlier that Enoch saw Jesus in heaven before creation and here are a couple reports of what he saw:

> And at that hour that Son of Man was named in the presence of the Lord of spirits, and His name was brought before the Head of Days. Even before the sun and the signs were created, before the stars of heaven were made, His name was named before the Lord of spirits [Colossians 1:15–17]. He shall be a Staff to the righteous and they shall steady themselves and not fall. And He shall be the Light of the Gentiles [Isaiah 49:6 and John 8:12], and the Hope of those who are troubled of heart...For He is mighty in all the secrets of righteousness, and unrighteousness shall disappear like a shadow, and will no longer exist; because the Elect One stands before the Lord of spirits, and His glory is for ever and ever, and His might for all generations. In Him dwells the spirit of wisdom, and the spirit which gives insight, and the spirit of understanding and of might, and the spirit of those who have fallen asleep in righteousness. And He shall judge the secret things, and no one shall be able to utter a lying or idle word before Him, for He is the Elect One before the Lord of spirits according to His good pleasure...And in those days shall the earth also give back that which has been entrusted to it, and Sheol also shall give back that which it has received, and hell shall give back that which it owes [1 Thessalonians 4:13–18]. For in those days the Elect One shall arise; And He shall choose the righteous and holy from among them. For the day has drawn near that they should be saved. And in those days the Elect One shall sit on His throne, and all the secrets of wisdom and counsel shall pour from His mouth, for the Lord of spirits hath given them to Him and has glorified Him [1 John 1:1–5].[1]
> (Lumpkin, *Enoch*, 81–85)

And the Head of Days came with Michael and Gabriel, Raphael and Phanuel, and thousands and ten thousands of angels without number [Revelation 5:11]. And the angel came to me and greeted me with his voice, and said to me: 'This is the Son of Man who is born to righteousness, and righteousness abides over Him, and the righteousness of the Head of Days forsakes Him not' [John 1:14]. And he said to me: 'He proclaims to you peace in the name of the world to come; for from there peace has proceeded since the creation of the world, and it shall be with you for ever and for ever and ever. And all shall walk in His ways since righteousness never forsook Him. Their dwelling place shall be with Him and it will be their heritage, and they shall not be separated from Him foe ever and ever and ever. And so there shall be length of days with the Son of Man, and the righteous shall have peace [Hebrews 4:3] and an upright way in the name of the Lord of spirits for ever and ever [John 17:24].'[2] (Lumpkin, *Enoch*, 122–123)

The name of Jesus is power, and every created thing will bow to Him at the end of the world. Philippians 2:9–11 says, "Therefore God also has highly exalted Him and given Him the name which is above every name, that at the name of Jesus every knee should bow, of those in heaven, and of those on earth, and of those under the earth, and that every tongue should confess that Jesus Christ is Lord, to the glory of God the Father." Jesus also goes by other names and here is what Isaiah 9:6 says, "For unto us a Child is born, unto us a Son is given; and the government will be upon His shoulder. And His name will be called Wonderful, Counselor, Mighty God, Everlasting Father, Prince of Peace" [Acts 4:12, Mark 16:17, and John 14:3].

HIS Sacrifice & HIS Salvation

Exodus 12:21–27 states:

"Then Moses called for all the elders of Israel and said to them, 'Pick out and take lambs for yourselves according to your families, and kill the Passover lamb. And you shall take a bunch of hyssop, dip it in the blood that is in the basin, and strike the lintel and the two doorposts with the blood that is in the basin. And none of you shall go out of the door of his house until morning. For the Lord will pass through to strike the Egyptians; and when He sees the blood on the lintel and on the two doorposts, the Lord will pass over the door and not allow the destroyer to come into your houses to strike you. And you shall observe this thing as an ordinance for you and your sons forever. It will come to pass when you come to the land which the Lord will give you, just as He promised, that you shall keep this service. And it shall be, when your children say to you, 'What do you mean by this service?', that you shall say, 'It is the Passover sacrifice of the Lord, who passed over the houses of the children of Israel in Egypt when He struck the Egyptians and delivered our households.' So the people bowed their heads and worshiped." (NKJV)

This would be fulfilled through Jesus, the Lamb of God, as Paul writes in 1 Corinthians 5:7, "Therefore purge out the old leaven, that you may be a new lump, since you truly are unleavened. For indeed Christ, our Passover, was sacrificed for us."

There are many other prophecies in the Hebrew Bible about the coming Messiah, His death, His resurrection, and His salvation. Jesus fulfilled all of them. We must remember that Paul called Jesus the last Adam in 1 Corinthians 15:45, "And so it is written, 'The first man Adam became a living being.' The last Adam became a life-giving spirit." The question is, were there others about this same Jesus that is not found in the Old Testament? The answer might be yes and here are several given directly to Adam from the Word (Jesus). I am going to call these Word (Jesus) to Adam moments.

Word (Jesus) to Adam:

But God the Lord said to Adam, 'I say to you, indeed, this darkness will pass from you every day, I have determined for you until the fulfillment of My covenant when I will save you and bring you back again into the garden and into the house of light you long for, in which there is no darkness. I will bring you to it in the kingdom of heaven'. Again God said to Adam, 'All this misery that you have been made to take on yourself because of your transgression will not free you from the hand of satan and it will not save you. But I will. When I shall come down from heaven and shall become flesh of your descendants [Luke 3:23–38], and take on Myself the infirmity from which you suffer then the darkness that covered you in this cave shall cover Me in the grave, when I am in the flesh of your descendants [John 1:14]. And I, who am without years, shall be subject to the reckoning of years of times of months, and of days, and I shall be reckoned as one of the sons of men in order to save you'.[3] (Lumpkin, *Adam & Eve*, 23–24)

Word (Jesus) to Adam:

Then the Word (Jesus) from God came to Adam, and said to him, 'You must know and understand concerning this satan, that he seeks to deceive you and your descendants after you'. And Adam cried before the Lord God, and begged and prayed to Him to give him something from the garden, as a token to him, wherein to be comforted... And when Adam saw the golden rods, the incense and the myrrh, he rejoiced and cried because he thought that the gold was a token of the kingdom from where he had come and the incense was a token of the bright light which had been taken from him, and that the myrrh was a token of the sorrow which he was in. After these things happened, God said to Adam, 'You asked Me for something from the garden to be comforted with, and I have given you these three tokens as a consolation to you so that you trust in Me and in My covenant with you. For I will come and save you and when I am in the flesh, kings shall bring Me gold, incense, and myrrh [Matthew 2:11]. Gold is a token of My kingdom, incense is a token of My divinity, and myrrh is a token of My suffering and of My death. But, Adam, put these by you in the cave, the gold so that it may shine light over you by night, the incense so that you smell its sweet savor, and the myrrh to comfort you in your sorrow'. When Adam heard these words from God, he worshipped before Him. He and Eve worshipped Him and gave Him thanks because He had dealt mercifully with them...God gave these three things to Adam on third day after he had come out of the garden as a sign of the three days the Lord should remain in the heart of the earth [Matthew 12:38–40]. And these three things, as they continued with Adam in the cave, gave him light by night, and by day they gave him a little relief from his sorrow.[4] (Lumpkin, *Adam & Eve*, 40–44)

We can read in Matthew 2:9–11, "When they heard the king, they departed; and behold, the star which they had seen in the East went before them, till it came and stood over where the young Child was. When they saw the star, they rejoiced with exceedingly great joy. And when they had come into the house, they saw the young Child with Mary His mother, and fell down and worshiped Him. And when they had opened their treasures, they presented gifts to Him: gold, frankincense, and myrrh."

Job 19:23–27 says, "Oh, that my words were written! Oh, that they were inscribed in a book! That they were engraved on a rock with an iron pen and lead, forever! For I know that my Redeemer lives, and He shall stand at last on the earth; and after my skin is destroyed, this I know, that in my flesh I shall see God, whom I shall see for myself, and my eyes shall behold, and not another. How my heart yearns within me!"

Word (Jesus) to Adam:

'And this sign, O Adam, will happen to Me at My coming on earth: satan will raise the people of the Jews to put me to death and they will lay Me in a rock, and seal a large stone over Me, and I shall remain within that rock three days and three nights. But on the third day I shall rise again [Mark 16:1–7], and it shall be salvation to you, O Adam, and to your decendants, so that you will believe in Me [Joel 2:32, Luke 9:21–22, and Romans 10:11–13]. But, Adam, I will not bring you from under this rock until three days and three nights have passed [Mark 14:1–72].'[5] (Lumpkin, *Adam & Eve*, 66–67)

We can read Peter's words in Acts 2:22–24, "'Men of Israel, hear these words: Jesus of Nazareth, a Man attested by God to you by miracles, wonders, and signs which God did through Him in your midst, as you yourselves also know – Him, being delivered by the determined purpose and foreknowledge of God, you have taken by lawless hands, have crucified, and put to death; whom God raised up, having loosed the pains of death, because it was not possible that He should be held by it'." Again in Acts 3:11–16,

"Now as the lame man who was healed held on to Peter and John, all the people ran together to them in the porch which is called Solomon's, greatly amazed. So when Peter saw it, he responded to the people: 'Men of Israel, why do you marvel at this? Or why look so intently at us, as though by our own power or godliness we made this man walk? The God of Abraham, Isaac, and Jacob, the God of our fathers, glorified His Servant Jesus, whom you delivered up and denied in the presence of Pilate, when he was determined to let him go. But you denied the Holy One and the Just, and asked for a murderer to be granted to you, and killed the Prince of Life, whom God raised from the dead, of which we are witnesses. And His name, through faith in His name, has made this man strong, whom you see and know. Yes, the faith which comes through Him has given him this perfect soundness in the presence of you all'." (NKJV)

Word (Jesus) to Adam:

> Then satan hurried with the sharp iron-stone he had and pierced Adam on the right side, and blood and water flowed. Then Adam fell on the altar like a corpse, and satan fled. Then Eve came and took Adam and placed him below the altar. There she stayed, crying over him while a stream of blood flowed from Adam's side over his offering. But God looked at the death of Adam. He then sent His Word and raised him up. And He said to him, 'Fulfill your offering because, certainly Adam, it is worthy and there is no imperfection in it'. God continued speaking to Adam, 'Thus will it also happen to Me while on the earth, when I shall be pierced [Zechariah 12:10] and blood and water shall flow from My side and run over My body, which is the true offering, and which shall be offered on the altar as a perfect offering'.[6] (Lumpkin, *Adam & Eve*, 99)

John 19:31–37 states,

> "Therefore, because it was the Preparation Day, that the bodies should not remain on the cross on the Sabbath (for that Sabbath was a high day), the Jews asked Pilate that their legs might be broken, and that they might be taken away. Then the soldiers came and broke the legs of the first and the other who was crucified with Him. But when they came to Jesus and saw that He was already dead, they did not break His legs. But one of the soldiers pierced His side with a spear, and immediately blood and water came out. And he who has seen has testified, and his testimony is true; and he knows that he is telling the truth, so that you may believe. For these things were done that the Scripture should be fulfilled, 'not one of His bones shall be broken'.

And again another Scripture says, 'they shall look on Him whom they pierced'." (NKJV)

Word (Jesus) to Adam:

Then the Word (Jesus) of God came to Adam, and said to him: 'Adam, you said, 'Bring me into a land where there is rest'. Another land than this will not bring you rest. It is the kingdom of heaven alone where there is rest. But you cannot enter into it at present, but only after your judgment is past and fulfilled. Then will I make you go up into the kingdom of heaven, you and your righteous descendants; and I will give you and them the rest that you ask for now [Matthew 11:28–29]. And if you said, 'Give me of the Water of Life that I may drink and live', it cannot be this day, but on the day that I shall descend into hell, and break the gates of brass, and crush into pieces the kingdoms of iron. Then I will, through mercy, save your soul and the souls of the righteous, and thus give them rest in My garden. That shall be when the end of the world is come. And the Water of Life you seek will not be granted you this day, but on the day that I shall shed My blood on your head in the land of Golgotha [Matthew 27:33, Mark 15:22, and John 19:17]. For My blood shall be the Water of Life to you at that time, and not to just you alone but to all your descendants who shall believe in Me [1 John 5:6]. This will be rest to them for forever'.[7] (Lumpkin, *Adam & Eve*, 56–57)

Leviticus 17:11 says, "'For the life of the flesh is in the blood, and I have given it to you upon the altar to make atonement for your souls; for it is the blood that makes atonement for the soul'." Jesus is the blood sacrifice for our souls as Matthew 26:28 states, "'For this is My blood of the new covenant, which is shed for many for the remission of sins'."

Word (Jesus) to Adam:

Then the Word (Jesus) of God came to Adam, and said to him, 'O Adam, as you have shed your blood so will I shed My own blood when I become flesh of your descendants. And as you died, O Adam, so also will I die. And as you built an altar, so also will I make for you an altar of the earth. And as you offered your blood on it, so also will I offer My blood on an altar on the earth. And as you appealed for forgiveness through that blood, so also will I make My blood forgiveness of sins, and erase transgressions in it [Matthew 26:27–28 and Revelation 1:5]. And now, behold, I have accepted your offering, O Adam, but the days of the covenant in which I have bound you are not fulfilled. When they are fulfilled, then will I bring you back into the garden [Luke 23:42–43]. Now, therefore, strengthen your heart. And when sorrow comes over you make Me an offering and I will be favorable to you'. But God knew that Adam believed he would frequently kill himself and make an offering to Him of his blood. Therefore He said to him, 'Adam, don't ever kill yourself like this again, by throwing yourself down from that mountain'. But Adam said to God, 'I was thinking to put an end to myself right now for having transgressed Your commandments and for my having come out of the beautiful garden and for the bright light which You have taken from me, and for the praises which poured out from my mouth without ceasing, and for the light that covered me. Yet because of Your goodness, O God, you did not get rid of me altogether, but you have been favorable to me every time I die and You bring me to life. And thereby it will be made known that You are a merciful God who does not want anyone to perish, who would love it if no one should fall, and who does not condemn anyone cruelly, badly, and by total destruction'. Then Adam remained silent. And the Word (Jesus) of God came to him and blessed him and comforted him and covenanted with him that He would save him at the end of the days determined for him. This, then, was the first offering Adam made to God and so it became his custom to do.[8] (Lumpkin, *Adam & Eve*, 33–35)

God said also to Adam, 'See this fire kindled by satan around your cave? See this curious thing that surrounds you? Know that it will surround both you and your descendants when you obey his command and he will plague you with fire and you will go down into hell after you are dead. Then, you will experience the burning of his fire that will surround you and your descendants. You will not be delivered from it until My coming. Just as you cannot go into your cave right now because of the great fire around it, a way for you will not be made for you until My Word (Jesus) comes on the day My covenant is fulfilled. There is no way for you at present to come from this life to rest until He who is My Word (Jesus) comes. Then He will make a way for you, and you shall have rest'. Then God called to the fire that burned around the cave with His Word (Jesus), that it spilt itself in half until Adam had passed through it. Then the fire parted itself by God's order and a way was made for Adam.[9] (Lumpkin, *Adam & Eve*, 61–62)

A way was also made for Moses and the Israelites on their way out of Egypt when God parted the waters so that they could pass though [Exodus 14]. God continues speaking to Adam, "However, when the covenant is fulfilled then I will show you and your descendants mercy, and bring you into a land of gladness where there is neither sorrow nor suffering but abiding joy and gladness, and light that never fails, and praises that never cease, and a beautiful garden that shall never pass away"[10] [Revelation 21:1–4 and 23].

HIS Judgment & HIS Kingdom

Psalm 110 states, "The Lord said to my Lord, 'Sit at My right hand, till I make Your enemies Your footstool'. The Lord shall send the rod of Your strength out of Zion. Rule in the midst of Your enemies! Your people shall be volunteers in the day of Your power; in the beauties of holiness, from the womb of the morning, You have the dew of Your youth. The lord has sworn and will not relent, 'You are a priest forever according to the order of Melchizedek'. The Lord is at Your right hand; He shall execute kings in the day of His wrath. He shall judge among the nations, He shall fill the places with dead bodies, He shall execute the heads of many countries. He shall drink of the brook by the wayside; therefore He shall lift up the head."

Here are several of Enoch's visions and prophecies concerning Jesus when He judges and His future kingdom:

> And there I saw One whose face looked ancient. His head was white like wool [Revelation 1:14], and with Him was another being whose countenance had the appearance of a man, and His face was full of graciousness, like one of the holy angels. And I asked the angel who went with me and showed me all the hidden things, concerning that Son of Man, who He was, and where He came from, and why He went with the Ancient One? And he answered and said to me: 'This is the Son of Man who hath righteousness, with whom dwell righteousness, and who reveals all the treasures of that which is hidden, because the Lord of spirits hath chosen Him, and whose lot has preeminence before the Lord of spirits in righteousness and is for ever. And this Son of Man whom you have seen shall raise up the kings and the mighty from their seats, and the strong from their thrones and shall loosen the reins of the strong, and break the teeth of the sinners. And He shall put down the kings from their thrones and kingdoms because they do not exalt and praise Him, nor humbly acknowledge who bestowed their kingdom on them. And He shall make the strong hang their heads, and shall fill them

with shame. And darkness shall be their dwelling, and worms shall be their bed, and they shall have no hope of rising from their beds, because they do not exalt the name of the Lord of spirits [Matthew 25:31–46].'[11] (Lumpkin, *Enoch*, 78–79)

Thus the Lord commanded the kings and the mighty and the exalted, and those who dwell on the earth, and said: 'Open your eyes and lift up your horns if you are able to recognize the Elect One'. And the Lord of spirits seated Him on the throne of His glory, and the spirit of righteousness was poured out on Him, and the word of His mouth slays all the sinners [Revelation 19:15–16], and all the unrighteous are destroyed from in front of His face. And in that day all the kings and the mighty, and the exalted and those who hold the earth shall stand up and shall see and recognize that He sits on the throne of His glory, and that righteousness is judged before Him, and no lying word is spoken before Him. Then pain will come on them as on a woman in labor [Isaiah 13:8]... And one portion of them shall look at the other, and they shall be terrified, and they shall look downcast, and pain shall seize them, when they see that Son of Man sitting on the throne of His glory. And the kings and the mighty and all who possess the earth shall bless and glorify and exalt Him who rules over all, who was hidden [Matthew 13:10–17]. For from the beginning the Son of Man was hidden, and the Most High preserved Him in the presence of His might, and revealed Him to the elect[Matthew 16:13–17].[12] (Lumpkin, *Enoch*, 102–104)

'On that day My Elect One shall sit on the throne of glory and shall try the works of the righteous, and their places of rest shall be innumerable. And their souls shall grow strong within them when they see My Elect One, and those who have called on My glorious name: Then will I

cause My Elect One to dwell among them. I will transform
heaven and make it an eternal blessing and light, and I
will transform the earth and make it a blessing, and I
will cause My elect ones to dwell on it. But the sinners
and evil-doers shall not set foot on it [Revelation 21].'[13]
(Lumpkin, *Enoch*, 78)

And in those days a whirlwind carried me off from the
earth [2 Kings 2:11], and set me down at the end of
heaven. There I saw another vision, the dwelling places of
the holy, and the resting places of the righteous. Here my
eyes saw the dwelling places of His righteous angels, and
the resting places of the holy ones. And they petitioned
and interceded and prayed for the children of men, and
righteousness flowed before them like water, and mercy
fell like dew on the earth: Thus it is among them for ever
and ever. And in that place my eyes saw the Elect One
of righteousness and of faith, and I saw His dwelling
place under the wings of the Lord of spirits [Matthew
26:64]. And righteousness shall prevail in His days, and
the righteous and elect shall be innumerable and will be
before Him for ever and ever. And all the righteous and
elect ones before Him shall be as bright as fiery lights,
and their mouth shall be full of blessing, and their lips
shall praise the name of the Lord of spirits. Righteousness
and truth before Him shall never fail. There I wished to
dwell, and my spirit longed for that dwelling place; and
thus it was decided and my portion was assigned and
established by the Lord of spirits. In those days I praised
and exalted the name of the Lord of spirits with blessings
and praises, because He had destined me for blessing
and glory according to the good pleasure of the Lord
of spirits. For a long time my eyes looked at that place,
and I blessed Him and praised Him, saying: 'Blessed is
He, and may He be blessed from the beginning and for
evermore. And in His presence there is no end. He knows

before the world was created what is for ever and what will be from generation to generation' [Revelation 4 and 5].[14] (Lumpkin, *Enoch*, 69–71)

Then I said: 'What is the purpose of this blessed land, which is entirely filled with trees, and what is the purpose of this accursed valley between them'? Then Uriel, one of the holy angels who was with me, answered and said: 'This accursed valley is for those who are cursed for ever: Here shall all the accursed be gathered together who utter with their lips words against the Lord not befitting His glory or say hard things against Him. Here shall they be gathered together, and here shall be their place of judgment. In the last days there shall be the spectacle of righteous judgment on them in the presence of the righteous for ever: here shall the merciful bless the Lord of glory, the Eternal King. In the days of judgment they shall bless Him for the mercy in that He has shown them' [Revelation 20:11–15].[15] (Lumpkin, *Enoch*, 61)

And he began his story saying: Enoch a righteous man, whose eyes were opened by God, saw the vision of the Holy One in heaven, which the angels showed me, and I heard everything from them, and I saw and understood, but it was not for this generation, but for a remote one which is to come. Concerning the elect I said, as I began my story concerning them: The Holy Great One will come out from His dwelling [Revelation 1:7], and the eternal God will tread on the earth, even on Mount Sinai, and appear in strength of His might from heaven. And all shall be very afraid, and the Watchers shall shake, and great fear and trembling shall seize them to the ends of the earth [Revelation 6:15]. And the high mountains shall be shaken, and the high hills shall be made low, and shall melt like wax in the flame. And the earth shall be wholly torn apart, and all that is on the earth shall be destroyed, and there shall be a judgment on all. But with the righteous He will make peace; and will protect the elect and mercy shall be on them. And they shall all belong to God, and they shall prosper, and they shall be blessed. And the light of God shall shine on them. And behold! He comes with ten thousand of His holy ones to execute judgment on all, and to destroy all the ungodly; and to convict all flesh of all the works of their ungodliness which they have ungodly committed, and of all the hard things which ungodly sinners have spoken against Him.[16] (Lumpkin, *Enoch*, 21–22)

In the words of Jesus Himself as stated in John 5:24–30:

"Most assuredly, I say to you, he who hears My word and believes in Him who sent Me has everlasting life, and shall not come into judgment, but has passed from death into life. Most assuredly, I say to you, the hour is coming, and now is, when the dead will hear the voice of the Son of God; and those who hear will live. For as the Father has life in Himself, so He has granted the Son to have life in Himself, and has given Him authority to execute judgment also, because He is the Son of Man. Do not marvel at this; for the hour is coming in which all who are in the graves will hear His voice and come forth – those who have done good, to the resurrection of life, and those who have done evil, to the resurrection of condemnation. I can of Myself do nothing. As I hear, I judge; and My judgment is righteous, because I do not seek My own will but the will of the Father who sent Me." (NKJV)

Lesser-Known Prophecy #1

I would like to thank Trey Smith of godinanutshell.com for this first one. We now know that Eve was deceived into eating of the fruit of the tree of knowledge of good and evil. Here is the Bible's account found in Genesis 3:1–6:

> "Now the serpent was more cunning than any beast of the field which the Lord God had made. And he said to the woman, 'Has God indeed said, 'You shall not eat of every tree of the garden'?' And the woman said to the serpent, 'We may eat the fruit of the trees of the garden; but of the fruit of the tree which is in the midst of the garden, God has said, 'You shall not eat it, nor shall you touch it. Lest you die'.' Then the serpent said to the woman, 'You will not surely die. For God knows that in the day you eat of it your eyes will be opened, and you will be like God, knowing good and evil'.' So when the woman saw that tree was good for food, that it was pleasant to the eyes, and a tree desirable to make one wise, she took of its fruit and ate. She also gave to her husband with her, and he ate." (NKJV)

I can only imagine what was going through the mind of Adam at this exact moment. On the one hand, God had told him, before Eve was even created out of Adam, that he should not eat of that fruit [Genesis 2:16–17] lest he die. On the other hand, here was Eve, created out of him and a part of him, his wife. I believe that Adam knew exactly what he was doing in that moment. Adam did not act out of defiance, but out of love. You see, he chose his wife, and his love for her, over everything, including God Himself. Adam chose to lay down his life for his bride. He chose death over life. What Adam could never do for Eve, God would do for all mankind, through His Son Jesus. Jesus did the exact same thing for His bride, the church. He chose to enter this world full of sin and become sin for all who would believe on Him. Jesus chose to leave His righteousness and glory in heaven to come down and be the perfect sacrifice that needed to happen so that we can be reconciled to God.

Lesser-Known Prophecy #2

We now know that the ark came to rest on the mountains of Ararat. Here is the Bible's account found in Genesis 8:1–4:

> "Then God remembered Noah, and every living thing, and all the animals that were with him in the ark. And God made a wind to pass over the earth, and the waters subsided. The fountains of the deep and the windows of heaven were also stopped, and the rain from heaven was restrained. And the waters receded continually from the earth. At the end of the hundred and fifty days the waters decreased. Then the ark rested in the seventh month, the seventeenth day of the month, on the mountains of Ararat." (NKJV)

So, the ark rested on the 17th day in the month of Nisan. Could there be another link to this date? Let us find out and go back in time to when the Israelites, or Hebrews, were freed from the bonds of slavery in Egypt and are now in the desert. The month of Nisan is now known as the first month of the Jewish new year because it is when they left Egypt. We must note that the Jewish calendar is a lunar calendar and not Gregorian, meaning their calendar is based on the cycles of the moon. Their days begin at twilight, when the sun is setting, and the moon has shown her face. We can read in Leviticus 23:4–11:

> "'These are the feasts of the Lord, holy convocations which you shall proclaim at their appointed times. On the fourteenth day of the first month at twilight is the Lord's Passover [Exodus 12]. And on the fifteenth day of the same month is the Feast of Unleavened Bread to the Lord [John 6:32–35]; seven days you must eat unleavened bread. On the first day you shall have a holy convocation; you shall do no customary work on it. But you shall offer an offering made by fire to the Lord for seven days. The seventh day shall be a holy convocation;

you shall do no customary work on it'. And the Lord spoke to Moses, saying, 'Speak to the children of Israel, and say to them: 'When you come into the land which I give to you, and reap its harvest, then you shall bring a sheaf of the firstfruits of your harvest to the priest. He shall wave the sheaf before the Lord, to be accepted on your behalf; on the day after the Sabbath the priest shall wave it'." (NKJV)

The priest would sacrifice the Passover lamb on the 14th of Nisan, and three days later, on the 17th of Nisan, the Feast of Firstfruits is celebrated. Did you know that Jesus Christ was crucified before the Passover celebration was to begin, on the 14th of Nisan, and would walk out of the tomb three days later just as He said He would, on the 17th of Nisan, during the firstfruit celebration?! Matthew 12:38–40 reads, "Then some of the scribes and Pharisees answered, saying, 'Teacher, we want to see a sign from You.' But He answered and said to them, 'An evil and adulterous generation seeks after a sign, and no sign will be given to it except the sign of the prophet Jonah. For as Jonah was three days and three nights in the belly of the great fish, so will the Son of Man be three days and three nights in the heart of the earth'."

The 17th of Nisan is when the ark rested from God's judgment and destruction through the flood. The 17th of Nisan is when Jesus Christ rose from the dead to give all who believe in Him rest for eternity. Matthew 11:25–30 reads:

"At that time Jesus answered and said, 'I thank You, Father, Lord of heaven and earth, that You have hidden these things from the wise and prudent and have revealed them to babes. Even so, Father, for so it seemed good in Your sight. All things have been delivered to Me by My Father, and no one knows the Son except the Father. Nor does anyone know the Father except the Son, and the one to whom the Son wills to reveal Him. Come to Me, all you who labor and are heavy laden, and I will give you rest. Take My yoke upon you and learn from Me, for I am gentle and lowly in heart, and you will find rest for your souls. For My yoke is easy and My burden is light'." (NKJV)

Only a God of love can do this! Only a God who is Creator of all can do this! What an amazing God I serve!!! Hopefully, after reading this amazing story of redemption and sacrifice, you too will now call on the name of Jesus to come into your heart and save you from eternal flames of fire and ice. My prayer is that in some form or fashion, this book has helped you understand that there is a God who is at work and never sleeps. He has been working ever since day one of Creation, and His Hand is all over HiStory. May He bless you and keep you! I love each and every one of you, but He loves you even more!!

End Notes

Preface

1   Joseph B. Lumkin, ed., *The Books of Enoch: The Complete Volume Containing: 1 Enoch (The Ethiopic Book of Enoch); 2 Enoch (The Slavonic Secrets of Enoch); 3 Enoch (The Hebrew Book of Enoch),* (Blountsville, AL (USA): Fifth Estate Publishers, 2010), pg. 5.

2   Ken Johnson, Th.D., ed., and R.H. Charles, trans., 1917 edition, *Ancient Book of Jubilees,* (United States of America: Biblefacts Ministries, 2013), pg. 5-6.

3   Rutherford H. Platt, ed., *The Forgotten Books of Eden,* (Lexington, KY (USA): 2016), pg. 1-2.

4   Louis Ginzberg, *The Legends of the Jews,* (Griot Publications, 2016), pg. 3.

5   Ken Johnson, Th.D., ed., *Ancient Book of Jasher: Referenced in Joshua 10:13; 2 Samuel 1:18; and 2 Timothy 3:8,* (United States of America: Biblefacts Ministries, 2008), pg. 4-5.

6   Joseph B. Lumpkin, ed., *The Books of Enoch: The Complete Volume Containing: 1 Enoch (The Ethiopic Book of Enoch); 2 Enoch (The Slavonic Secrets of Enoch; 3 Enoch (The Hebrew Book of Enoch),* (Blountsville, AL (USA): Fifth Estate Publishers, 2010), pg.11-12.

7   Kurt P. Wise, *Faith, Form, and Time: What the Bible Teaches and Science Confirms About Creation and the Age of the Universe,* (Nashville, TN (USA): B&H Publishing Group, 2002), pg. 26.

Introduction

1   Paul G. Humber, ed., *Reasons to Affirm a Global Flood,* 2nd edition, (2013), pg. 25.

2   Ibid, pg. 22.

3   Ibid, pg. 24.

4   Ibid, pg. 10.

5   Ibid, pg. 8.

6   Ibid, pg. 5-6.

7   Ibid, pg. 5.

8   Ibid, pg. 26.

9   Ibid, pg. 1.

10 Ibid, pg. 19-20.

11 Ibid, pg. 1.

12 Ibid, pg. 26.

Creation and the Fall

1   "Norse Mythology", Emma Groeneveld, Ancient History Encyclopedia, Last modified November 02, 2017, Accessed May 01, 2020, https://www.ancient. eu/Norse_Mythology/.

2   "Enuma Elish – The Babylonian Epic of Creation – Full Text", Joshua J. Mark, Ancient History Encyclopedia, Last modified May 04, 2018, Accessed May 01, 2020, https://www.ancient.eu/article/225/.

3   Kurt P. Wise, *Faith, Form, and Time: What the Bible Teaches and Science Confirms About Creation and the Age of the Universe*, (Nashville, TN (USA): B&H Publishing Group, 2002), pg. 5.

4   Ibid, pg. 34-35.

5   Ken Johnson, Th.D., ed., *Ancient Book of Jasher: referenced in Joshua 10:13; 2 Samuel 1:18; and 2 Timothy 3:8*, (United States of America: Biblefacts Ministries, 2008), pg. 7.

6   Ken Johnson, Th.D., ed., and R.H. Charles, trans., 1917 edition, *Ancient Book of Jubilees*, (United States of America: Biblefacts Ministries, 2013), pg. 15-17.

7   Joseph B. Lumpkin, ed., *The First and Second Books of Adam and Eve: The Conflict with Satan*, (Blountsville, AL (USA): Fifth Estate Publishers, 2009), pg. 8.

8   Louis Ginzberg, *The Legends of the Jews*, (Griot Publications, 2016), pg. 20.

9   Ibid, pg. 21.

10 Ibid, pg. 24-25.

11 Ibid, pg. 27.

12 Ibid, pg. 21-22.

13 Joseph B. Lumpkin, ed., *The Books of Enoch: The Complete Volume Containing: 1 Enoch (The Ethiopic Book of Enoch); 2 Enoch (The Slavonic Secrets of Enoch); 3 Enoch (The Hebrew Book of Enoch)*, (Blountsville, AL (USA): Fifth Estate Publishers, 2010), pg. 277.

14 Louis Ginzberg, *The Legends of the Jews*, (Griot Publications, 2016), pg. 25.

15 Joseph B. Lumpkin, ed., *The Books of Enoch: The Complete Volume Containing: 1 Enoch (The Ethiopic Book of Enoch); 2 Enoch (The Slavonic Secrets of Enoch);*

3 Enoch (The Hebrew Book of Enoch), (Blountsville, AL (USA): Fifth Estate Publishers, 2010), pg. 96, 99.

16 Louis Ginzberg, *The Legends of the Jews*, (Griot Publications, 2016), pg. 15.

17 Ibid, pg. 14-15

18 Ibid, pg. 28.

19 Ken Johnson, Th.D., ed, and R.H. Charles, trans., 1917 edition, *Ancient Book of Jubilees*, (United States of America: Biblefacts Ministries, 2013), pg. 21-22.

20 Louis Ginzberg, *The Legends of the Jews*, (Griot Publications, 2016), pg. 30.

21 Ibid, pg. 30-31.

22 Ibid, pg. 30.

23 Ibid, pg. 31.

24 Ken Johnson, Th.D., ed., *Ancient Book of Jasher: Referenced in Joshua 10:13; 2 Samuel 1:18; and 2 Timothy 3:8*, (United States of America: Biblefacts Ministries, 2008), pg. 17.

Adam and Eve

1 Joseph B. Lumpkin, ed., *The First and Second Books of Adam and Eve: The Conflict with Satan*, (Blountsville, AL (USA): Fifth Estate Publishers, 2009), pg. 12.

2 Ibid, pg. 16-17.

3 Ibid, pg. 18.

4 Ibid, pg. 15-16.

5 Ibid, pg. 10.

6 Ibid, pg. 74-78

7 Ibid, pg. 14-15

8 Ibid, pg. 21-23

9 Ibid, pg. 25-27

10 Ibid, pg. 68-69.

11 Ibid, pg. 37-38.

12 Ibid, pg. 130-131.

Enoch, the Fallen Angels & Giants

1 Ken Johnson, Th.D., ed., and R.H. Charles, trans., 1917 edition, *Ancient Book of Jubilees*, (United States of America: Biblefacts Ministries, 2013), pg. 50.

2 Joseph B. Lumpkin, ed., *The Books of Enoch: The Complete Volume Containing: 1 Enoch (The Ethiopic Book of Enoch); 2 Enoch (The Slavonic Secrets of Enoch); 3 Enoch (The Hebrew Book of Enoch)*, (Blountsville, AL (USA): Fifth Estate Publishers, 2010), pg. 145-146.

3   Joseph B. Lumpkin, ed., *The First and Second Books of Adam and Eve: The Conflict with Satan*, (Blountsville, AL (USA):Fifth Estate Publishers, 2009), pg. 170.

4   Ken Johnson, Th.D., ed., and R.H. Charles, trans., 1917 edition, *Ancient Book of Jubilees*, (United States of America: Biblefacts Ministries, 2013), pg. 24-25.

5   Louis Ginzberg, *The Legends of the Jews*, (Griot Publications, 2016), pg. 47-48.

6   Ken Johnson, Th.D., ed., *Ancient Book of Jasher: Referenced in Joshua 10:13; 2 Samuel 1:18; and 2 Timothy 3:8*, (United States of America: Biblefacts Ministries, 2008), pg. 10.

7   Joseph B. Lumpkin, ed., *The Books of Enoch: The Complete Volume Containing: 1 Enoch (The Ethiopic Book of Enoch); 2 Enoch (The Slavonic Secrets of Enoch); 3 Enoch (The Hebrew Book of Enoch)*, (Blountsville, AL (USA): Fifth Estate Publishers, 2010), pg. 67-68.

8   Louis Ginzberg, *The Legends of the Jews*, (Griot Publications, 2016), pg. 46.

9   Joseph B. Lumpkin, ed., *The First and Second Books of Adam and Eve: The Conflict with Satan*, (Blountsville, AL (USA): Fifth Estate Publishers, 2009), pg. 171.

10   Ken Johnson, Th.D., ed., *Ancient Book of Jasher: referenced in Joshua 10:13; 2 Samuel 1:18; and 2 Timothy 3:8*, (United States of America: Biblefacts Ministries, 2008), pg. 11.

11   Ibid, pg. 11-12.

12   Joseph B. Lumpkin, ed., *The Books of Enoch: The Complete Volume Containing: 1 Enoch (The Ethiopic Book of Enoch); 2 Enoch (The Slavonic Secrets of Enoch); 3 Enoch (The Hebrew Book of Enoch)*, (Blountsville, AL (USA): Fifth Estate Publishers, 2010), pg. 284-285.

13   Ibid, pg. 151-153.

14   Ibid, pg. 26-30.

15   Louis Ginzberg, *The Legends of the Jews*, (Griot Publications, 2016), pg. 45.

16   Joseph B. Lumpkin, ed., *The Books of Enoch: The Complete Volume Containing: 1 Enoch (The Ethiopic Book of Enoch); 2 Enoch (The Slavonic Secrets of Enoch); 3 Enoch (The Hebrew Book of Enoch)*, (Blountsville, AL (USA): Fifth Estate Publishers, 2010), pg. 108-110.

17   Ken Johnson, Th.D., ed., and R.H. Charles, trans., 1917 edition, *Ancient Book of Jubilees*, (United States of America: Biblefacts Ministries, 2013), pg. 28.

18   Joseph B. Lumpkin, ed., *The Books of Enoch: The Complete Volume Containing: 1 Enoch (The Ethiopic Book of Enoch); 2 Enoch (The Slavonic Secrets of Enoch); 3 Enoch (The Hebrew Book of Enoch)*, (Blountsville, AL (USA): Fifth Estate Publishers, 2010), pg. 39-41.

19   Ibid, pg. 44-47.

20   Ibid, pg. 30-35.

21   Ibid, pg. 88-89.

22   Ken Johnson, Th.D., ed., and R.H. Charles, trans., 1917 edition, *Ancient Book of Jubilees*, (United States of America: Biblefacts Ministries, 2013), pg. 39.

23 Louis Ginzberg, *The Legends of the Jews*, (Griot Publications, 2016), pg. 51.

24 Ibid, pg. 49-50.

Noah and the Great Flood

1   Louis Ginzberg, *The Legends of the Jews*, (Griot Publications, 2016), pg. 51.

2   Ken Johnson, Th.D., ed., *Ancient Book of Jasher: Referenced in Joshua 10:13; 2 Samuel 1:18; and 2 Timothy 3:8*, (United States of America: Biblefacts Ministries, 2008), pg. 13-14.

3   Ibid, pg. 13.

4   Louis Ginzberg, *The Legends of the Jews*, (Griot Publications, 2016), pg. 53.

5   Ken Johnson, Th.D., ed., *Ancient Book of Jasher: Referenced in Joshua 10:13; 2 Samuel 1:18; and 2 Timothy 3:8*, (United States of America: Biblefacts Ministries, 2008), pg. 14.

6   Ibid, pg. 12-13.

7   Ibid, pg. 14-15.

8   Ken Johnson, Th.D., ed., and R.H. Charles, trans., 1917 edition, *Ancient Book of Jubilees*, (United States of America: Biblefacts Ministries, 2013), pg. 28.

9   Ken Johnson, Th.D., ed., *Ancient Book of Jasher: Referenced in Joshua 10:13; 2 Samuel 1:18; and 2 Timothy 3:8*, (United State of America: Biblefacts Ministries, 2008), pg. 15.

10 Ken Johnson, Th.D., ed., and R.H. Charles, trans., 1917 edition, *Ancient Book of Jubilees*, (United States of America: Biblefacts Ministries, 2013), pg. 30.

11 Ken Johnson, Th.D., ed., *Ancient Book of Jasher: referenced in Joshua 10:13; 2 Samuel 1:18; and 2 Timothy 3:8*, (United States of America: Biblefacts Ministries, 2008), pg. 15-16.

12 Louis Ginzberg, *The Legends of the Jews*, (Griot Publications, 2016), pg. 56.

13 Joseph B. Lumpkin, ed., *The Books of Enoch: The Complete Volume Containing: 1 Enoch (The Ethiopic Book of Enoch); 2 Enoch (The Slavonic Secrets of Enoch); 3 Enoch (The Hebrew Book of Enoch)*, (Blountsville, AL (USA): Fifth Estate Publishers, 2010), pg. 211-214.

Jesus and the Prophecies

1   Joseph B. Lumpkin, ed., *The Books of Enoch: The Complete Volume Containing: 1 Enoch (The Ethiopic Book of Enoch); 2 Enoch (The Slavonic Secrets of Enoch); 3 Enoch (The Hebrew Book of Enoch)*, (Blountsville, AL (USA): Fifth Estate Publishers, 2010), pg. 81-85.

2   Ibid, pg. 122-123.

3   Joseph B. Lumpkin, ed., *The First and Second Books of Adam and Eve: The Conflict with Satan*, (Blountsville, AL (USA): Fifth Estate Publishers, 2009), pg. 23-24.

4   Ibid, pg. 40-44.

5   Ibid, pg. 66-67.

6   Ibid, pg. 99.

7   Ibid, pg. 56-57.

8   Ibid, pg. 33-35.

9   Ibid, pg. 61-62.

10   Ibid, pg. 36.

11   Joseph B. Lumpkin, ed., *The Books of Enoch: The Complete Volume Containing: 1 Enoch (The Ethiopic Book of Enoch); 2 Enoch (The Slavonic Secrets of Enoch); 3 Enoch (The Hebrew Book of Enoch)*, (Blountsville, AL (USA): Fifth Estate Publishers, 2010), pg. 78-79.

12   Ibid, pg. 102-104.

13   Ibid, pg. 78.

14   Ibid, pg. 69-71.

15   Ibid, pg. 61.

16   Ibid, pg. 21-22.

Bibliography

Ginzberg, Louis. *The Legends of the Jews*. Griot Publications, 2016.

Groeneveld, Emma. "Norse Mythology." *Ancient History Encyclopedia*. Last modified November 02, 2017. Accessed May 01, 2020. https://www. ancient.eu/Norse_Mythology/.

Humber, Paul G., ed. *Reasons to Affirm a Global Flood*. 2nd edition. 2013.

Johnson, Ken, Th.D. ed. *Ancient Book of Jasher: Referenced in Joshua 10:13; 2 Samuel 1:18; and 2 Timothy 3:8*. United States of America, Biblefacts Ministries, 2008.

Johnson, Ken, Th.D., ed. and R. H. Charles, trans., 1917 Edition. *Ancient Book of Jubilees*. United States of America, Biblefacts Ministries, 2013.

Lumpkin, Joseph B., ed. *The Books of Enoch: A Complete Volume Containing 1 Enoch (The Ethiopic Book of Enoch); 2 Enoch (The Slavonic Secrets of Enoch; 3 Enoch (The Hebrew Book of Enoch)*. Blountsville, AL (USA): Fifth Estate Publishers, 2010.

Lumpkin, Joseph B., ed. *The First and Second Books of Adam and Eve: The Conflict with Satan*. Blountsville, AL (USA): Fifth Estate Publishers, 2009.

Mark, Joshua J. "Enuma Elish – The Babylonian Epic of Creation – Full Text." *Ancient History Encyclopedia*. Last modified May 04, 2018. Accessed May 01, 2020. https://www.ancient.eu/article/225/.

Platt, Rutherford H., ed. *The Forgotten Books of Eden*. Lexington, KY (USA): 2016.

Wise, Kurt P. *Faith, Form, and Time: What the Bible Teaches and Science Confirms About Creation and the Age of the Universe*. Nashville, TN (USA): B&H Publishing Group, 2002.

Afterword

"Now **faith** is the substance of things hoped for, the evidence of things not seen. For by it the elders obtained a good testimony. By **faith** we understand that the worlds were framed by the Word of God, so that the things which are seen were not made of things which are visible. By **faith** Abel offered to God a more excellent sacrifice than Cain, through which he obtained witness that he was righteous, God testifying to his gifts; and through it he being dead still speaks. By **faith** Enoch was taken away so that he did not see death, 'and was not found, because God had taken him'; for before he was taken he had this testimony, that he pleased God. But without **faith** it is impossible to please Him, for he who comes to God must believe that He is, and that He is a rewarder of those who diligently seek Him. By **faith** Noah, being divinely warned of things not yet seen, moved with godly fear, prepared an ark for the saving of his household, by which he condemned the world and became heir of the righteousness which is according to faith." – Hebrews 11:1-7

Printed in the United States
by Baker & Taylor Publisher Services